Bill M Burton

Edited by Debbie L Burton

Other Works by
Author
Bill M Burton

Poetry
"Quotes of gratitude" (2017)
Paper back
E-book
Audio book
MP3

**"OUR STRUGGLES WILL
TEACH US HOW TO GROW" (2015)**
Paper back
E-book
Audio book
MP3

"POETRY IN ACTION" (2012)
Paper back
E-book
Audio book
MP3

"Quotes of gratitude"

Progressive and solutions

Bill M Burton

Edited by Debbie L Burton

Contents

Acknowledgements

Preface

Copyright   2017 by Bill M Burton

Burton Bill M 1959

Title: Quotes of gratitude

ISBN: 978-0-9918404-8-9

All rights reserved. No part of this publication may be reproduced or Transmitted, in any form or by any means, without the written consent of Burton Publishing

Edited by Debbie L Burton

Book covers design by digimaxcreative.com

Burton Publishing
111 St. Lucie Drive,
North York Ontario,
Canada, M9M 1T4

Web and Social Media
billburton@rogers.com
Mobile 647 860 7145
www.facebook.com/BurtonPublishing
https://twitter.com/BillMBurton

Acknowledgements

My gratitude goes out to Debbie L Burton my sister and editor who have worked with me for so many years; she holds an important part of the work that we are sharing with you today. To my children and my family thank you for caring so much. I say many thanks to Davey C Burton my son who formatted my new book "Our struggles will teach us how to grow. "He did a fantastic job creating the cover and uploading the book to Amazon.

A constant reminder from a long time friend Christopher Thomas, who stresses the significant of the book of poetry and the profit, it can give to the people who are willing to nurture a new way of life with its vigorous uplifting persuasions. Thanks to Sean Liburd of the Knowledge book store in Brampton 177 Queen ST.W Ontario Canada. Who has helped in the promotion of my books, "Poetry in action" and "our struggles will teach us how to grow". My appreciation to the Amazon team who have done such a wonderful job.

Thanks to all of the other writers who have paved the way that we can now share the knowledge that we enjoy today. I would like to thank all the book stores that showed so much love, support and guidance in my journey into the publishing world. Many thanks to my devoted fans who have purchase my work and believe. I want to share my gratefulness to such writers like Marcus Garvey, Bob Marley, Langston Hughes, Maya Angelou, Claude Mackay, Louise Bennett, Vernon Howard, Valorie Burton and James Allen.

Our appreciation to the higher powers that give us the strength to go the extra furlong so we can put this road map of wisdom to essential vocation. This endeavor is for those who are willing to utilize its unbiased contents of factual understanding that will show them the way to a most gracious life of happiness, harmony, a giving nature of unconditional love and respect to all people that inhabit the universe.

Bill M Burton

VII

Preface 1

When we encourage the tools from within our grasp, we can chip away at whatever we are planning to overcome. Our efforts will multiply beyond our wildest imagination, into the things that we have invested in. Everyone gets tired at some point in time, yet determination with its will power can drive us home safely with great intention in abundance to fulfill our desires.

As a songwriter, co-workers and friends suggested that my poetry could help many people to see that they all have potential in some way or another in life's journey. When we are weary from our daily work, we have to remember to see the whole picture in its absolute grandeur. Sometime our focus won't stay intact long enough that we can complete our task. Yet we must gather our strength in one doing action pact, setting sail once more in order to receive all that we dream about and work towards, in the spare time we have managed to put together.

We all need spiritual guidance to bridge the gap in all that exists in the universe, and then material things will have its practical avenue in all what we sought. The rationale of this book is to reach out to all who is in the frame of mind to do, encouraging them in whatever they might think is too difficult to tackle. When our task seems too complex to finish, there is always answers within our grasp, by getting a bit of rest then looking from a new angle, the answers will be waiting for us.

The people I have in mind to read or recite my poetry is whomever wishes to observe, learn and give back to society as a true whole. I have no intention of running away with the whole trophy and not sharing it with others. What kind of life can we enjoy if we don't give freely to all creatures without some unwanted strings attached? The love of life is the essence of living, sharing the possibilities with all nations that breathe here and now. Not for one single moment will I entertain the thought of belittling another soul to receive favors regardless of the bounty that could await my coffer.

Why I wrote about the awareness of poetry, is to remind the human race that all existence is a precious thing, when we start having favorites that is when we "drift" into a very deep sleep, never to be awakened. Remember misinformation is a dangerous, corrupted short-sighted missile that has no real friends. To be aware of the destruction that lies afar, can bring about the sanctuary of the innocents, that can really cleanse our twisted hearts. Yet sadly most of the world inhabitancies are in an abrasive degraded never ending circle of confusion. Go now and give freely to all creatures.

Bill M Burton

Preface 2

As we know, a real poet speaks heartily about life itself and what will draw us closer. Life teaches us on a daily basis the pros and cons, what to do and what not to do. My whole purpose of writing poetry is to share the knowledge to make life more livable for all who seeks it. Life experiences always educate the most crucial lesson. It's difficult to live under so much pressure, figuring out what to do next, making the right decision without falling through some awaiting dungeon that time has saved for us.

It is our given right to demand from our self what we really want and then go out there, cast our lines and reel in the big fish of the ocean.
Writing for me is a bit different from most writers I would write a song lyric then a poem or vice versa, whatever comes to mind. As a writer, rewrite is very important because you can always make your work stronger and clearer, in all cases a song must be understood by the second line.

The feeling of giving is what propels my life as a whole, knowing that my readers and listeners are getting all the passionate strength from the knowledge that I'm sharing, whether from the printed pages, song lyrics E-cards, E-books, MP3 or from my audio books. I have no appetite for the greediness that has most people, warped in so many unwanted desires that hurt the masses on such a weighty scale. It is true that the world needs more people to lift the burden off the shoulders of the sanction poor.

To get the most out of my work is through the understanding of the whole poem. It doesn't hurt to read the poem two or three times so you can appreciate the meaning of its full significance. From each reading of anyone of the poem, you will be surprised to know what you will discover each time. All the poems are written with calmness in mind of my readers, listeners and viewers with the purpose of reconnecting the quietness of life they might be missing.

The hardness of life pushes me to write every day. Therapeutically speaking, poetry lifted the numbness from my heart, gives me the power to carry on with my works that I have started more than twenty years ago. Poetry has the real antidote within its words of wisdom. Poetry doesn't need any artificial flavor to spruce it up to life form. It has the genuine substance that all living creatures need to stay alive. Poetry is Truth, Respect, Love, Honesty, Compassion and everlasting authentic confidence.

Bill M Burton

Confidence and desire

Confidence and desire

Confidence..2
Aspire..2
Our midst..2
Can succeed..2
Be done..3
The seeker..3
Next move..3
Drifting..3
Strength..4
End result..4
Desire..4
Keep on trying..4
Liberation..5
Trueness..5
To gain..5
A sparkle..5
Persisting..6
In due time..6
Your duty..6
Make me realize..6
Steady future..7
Elevating..7
Your want..7
Our dream..7
Genuine aspiration..8
Our upkeep..8
Inner core..8
Complete..8
Newness..9
Detour..9
Arise..9
Humbleness..9
Will change..10
To bestowed..10
Break the spell..10
Get out..10
Were perfect..11
A moment..11
Ease your mind..11
Share..11
Daffodil..11
Natural..11
Pure and true..11
Guidance..12

Confidence and desire

Stride 12
Precious love 12
Time 12
Gentleness 12
Sweetest love 13
New conclusion 13
Strength 13
Make amend 13
Ultimate 13
Enough time 14
Have to 14
Objective 14
Whole heart 14
Make a start 15
Gooder 15
Goodest 15
When 15
For you 16
Misgiving 16
Durability 16
Truly sublime 16
Watch as much 17
Listen 17
Until 17
Doing 17
Two steps 18
Our duty 18
Use of time 18
Awake 18
Learning how 19
Pursue 19
Enlighten 19
Stay away 19
On course 20
It's time 20
Refresh 20
Be employ 20
Make it 21
Why wait 21
Overdue 21
Satisfaction 21
True desire 22
New strategies 22
Objective 22
Revisit 22

Confidence and desire

Coax it back	23
Today's living	23
Sunshine	23
Test of time	23
Existence	24
Ideas	24
Adjust	24
A balance	24
Transpire	25
Achieve	25
Take the time	25
Lofty living	25
Induce	26
Already wired	26
Half way	26
You're duty	26
An aim	27
My life	27
Way out	27
Our will	27
Liberating	28
Perfect time	28
Fulfillment	28
Readiness	28
Small steps	29
Life of peace	29
Renew	29
Stand firm	29
Perseverance	30
On course	30
To achieve	30
Antidote	30
Biggest advertiser	31
Fruitful society	31
Progress	31
Pure love	31
Wake up	32
Uplifted	32
Complete	32
Guidance	32
The most	33
Lighthouse	33
What's overdue?	33

Confidence and desire

Success...33
See the idea..34
Get moving...34
Beyond..34
A price..34
Another Person...35
Full time...35
Bits and pieces...35
Your move..35
Wake you up..36
Definite solution..36
Until we see...36
Doing..36
Precision...37
Key message..37
Self-confidence..37
Solution..37
Determination..38
Dedication..38
Persistence...38
You're gate...38
Take control...39
Understand...39
Don't hesitate...39
Activate..39
Never mind..40
Life will..40
To believe..40
Start over...40
Satisfied...41
Worthwhile..41
Diamond platter..41
No one..41
To win..42
Above defeat...42
Readiness...42
Obstacles..42
Our thoughts..43
A flicker...43
Real handle..43
Consciousness...43
Impress...44
Ambush..44

Confidence and desire

Golden spoon...44
Graceful..44
Prosperous...45
Positive shift..45
Chances..45
Concise...45
Renewal..46
Silent killer..46
Solitude..46
Essential...46
"The world fastest"...47
Genuine..48
New avenue...48
Alert..48
Wiser...48
Greater...49
Persuasion...49
Doable passage...49
Fruition..49
Bounce back..50
Fresh outlook..50
First glow...50
Your policy..50
Unity...51
Devotion..51
Will grow...51
Sacred...51
Consistence...52
The reason...52
Explore...52
Give...52
The leader..53
Real power...53
Honesty..53
Act of love...53
Selected dream..53
Realizing..53
Avenues..54
Stamina..54
Revive...54
Out of exile..54
Steadily..54
Recuperate...54

XV

Confidence and desire

Laugher is free 55
Not in a bottle 55
Dependable 55
Happiness 55
Your will 56
Essence to build 56
Ultimate prize 56
Create and achieve 56

Determination

Determination

The doer	58
Can inflict	58
Furlong	58
Your side	58
Given gift	58
Golden spoon	58
How long	58
Has to pay	58
Into place	59
Humble giving	59
Be kept	59
Ride the waves	59
Times of need	59
Validate	59
Inside	60
Time to teach	60
Cross road	60
Take a stand	60
Such a test	60
Adapt	61
Face the facts	61
Just delayed	61
Sitting here	61
Own future	61
Comforting	61
Look beyond	62
Lump sum	62
Inside my heart	62
Duty	62
Loosen the knot	62
Be thirsty	63
A start	63
Lead thy self	63
Maturity	63
Trials and errors	63
Rise up	64
Long enough	64
Security	65
Venturing out	65
The ladder	66
Crave	66
The remedy	66
Go forth	66
Have to study	66

Determination

Trying..66
Can do...66
Multitudes...67
Grown up..67
Deliberate..67
Decisive...67
The drive...67
A new craft...68
Stay the course..68
Revisit...68
Flow of goals..68
Under wraps..69
Be on hand..69
Tardiness...69
Sweetness..69
Bonus of love..70
Persevere...70
Why wait...70
Worth..70
Pursue..71
Reserve..71
Pay our dues..71
Evoke..71
Greatest...72
Certain things..72
Endow...72
Unless..72
Fakeish applause...73
Baby steps...73
Faulty Smile..73
Our strength..73
Real sequence...74
Advantage...74
Confidence..74
Believing...74
Treasure..75
Mystical..75
Grove..75
Ingrain...75
Sophisticated...76
Rhythm...76
Chances..76
Our heart...76

Hardship

Hardship

Corrupted	78
Take from	78
To belittle	78
Diamond spoon	78
Same cage	79
Liquidated	79
Own tip	79
Near future	79
Be steady	80
Destroy	80
Renew	81
Design	81
Worldwide	81
Health	81
Moral duty	82
Dread	82
Lies	82
Dismantle	82
Illusion	82
New start	82
Don't waste	83
Stifled	83
Sour	83
Counts	83
Weary shells	84
Upper class	84
To cope	84
Mislead	84
Divide	84
Lowest	85
Destroy	85
The tattle	85
Cruel steam	85
Fruitless fake	86
Truth	86
Contradiction	86
Real you	86
Smarty pants	87
Weary	87
Certified	87
Duel	87
Greedier	88
Signs	88

Hardship

Bribe	88
Heartless	88
Sunshine	88
Remind	88
Suffocate	89
Safety	89
Change	89
Token	89
Cold-hearted	90
Displeasure	90
Deceptive	90
Suffered	90
Income	91
Pretending	91
Hardship	91
New rule	91
Nothing new	92
Perished	92
Over whelming	92
Foundation	92
Clutter	93
Be alert	93
Health	93
Arrive	93
Demand	94
Dress up	94
Protectors	94
Liberties	94
Discreetly	94
Color	95
Love	95
Broken	95
Manifested	95
Prefabricating	95
Security	95
Vitalizing	95
Unlawful	96
Destructive	96
Cruel sting	96
Destroy	96
Full conquest	97
Threshold	97
Bits and pieces	97

Hardship

Move..97
Under the strip..98
Two-face...98
Existence..98
Alertness..98
All colors..99
Harmony...99
Phrases...99
Enlighten..99
Elite..100
Easy pray..100
Rejuvenate..100
Overwork..100
First..101
Second..101
Third...101
Coffer...101
Already...102
Attention...102
Damage...102
Satisfaction...102
Treacherous..103
Damage...103
Seek..103
Rebound..103
Hazard..104
Bleaching..104
Recharge...104
Embrace..104
Stealing lyrics...105
Factory...105
Laziness..105
Smother..105
Careful...106
Foresight..106
Safely...106
Slow down..106
Clientele...107
Poorest...107
Hideous..107
Hurtful...107
Selfish flavor..108
Opposition..108

XXV

Hardship

Distance	108
Laughter	108
Wandering sieve	109
Noise	109
Bias king	109
Existence	109
Quickly	110
Concise	110
Seekers	110
Spies	110
Undesirable	110

XXVII

Sabotaging and deceit

XXVIII

Sabotaging and deceit

Conquers..112
Uppers...112
Hardly..112
Crumbling...112
Daze...112
Egos...112
Reclaim..113
Handle...113
Learned..113
Dim..113
Conceal..114
Rehearing..114
Lowly..114
Face...114
Often...114
Fresh start...114
Why damage...115
Fix...115
Minding...115
Hearsays..115
Ambush your speech..116
Constant..116
Swindling..116
Little ego...117
Petty security..117
Devour..117
Hardship...117
Children cry..118
Oneness..118
Destroyers..118
Preside..119
Certain..119
Cleaver...119
New faces...119
Trapped..120
Own plan..120
Persecuted..120
Concern..120
In your face..121
The loot..121
Remember..121
The light...121
Bend...122

XXIX

Sabotaging and deceit

No sense..122
Sides..122
Teach...122

XXXI

Preferential treatment

Preferential treatment

Select few	124
Itself	124
Why cast doubt	124
Are one	124
Fussy view	125
Happy	125
Scheme	125
Petition	125
Ultimate dream	126
Racism does kill	126
Attitude	126
So many colors	127
Listen	127
Existence	127
Vicious	127
To be strong	128
Sunshine	128
Capsize	128
Abound	128
Unkind brittle	129
Beauty	129
Unwanted	129
Universe	129
Black or white	130
They are	130
Myth	130
Realized	130
Dark-horse	131
Spots	131
Love	131
Began	131
Why labeled	132
Words	132
Respect	132
Effort	132
Disarm	133
Leave	133
Smear	133
Inserted	133
Favorites	134
Subside	134
Deceits	134
Head to toe	134

Preferential treatment

Deceitfulness	135
Confidence	135
New strength	135
Cultivate	135
Substance	136
Reasonable	136
Revive	136
Humbleness	136

XXXV

Love and respect

Love and respect

Teaches..138
Honest...138
Give..138
Courage..138
Upkeep...139
Strength...139
Fertile..139
Deserve..139
Mistaken..140
Leeway...140
Heart deep...140
Pleasant tune...141
Creed...141
Gift...141
Beacon...141
Purifies..142
Honeycomb..142
Can-do attitude...142
Your own..142
Look alike..143
Efficient..143
End result...143
Put away...143
To say...144
Honest face..144
Come and gone..144
Peaceful..144
Grace..145
Natural spring..145
Spunky persona...145
Potency...145
Shatters doubt..146
Up to par..146
Reunite...146
Right road..146
Chosen...147
I can see..147
Careful...147
The key 148
Little while..148
No one...148
Pure..148
Distant lure..149
My heart..149

XXXVII

Love and respect

Chancy...149
Ultimate task...149
Authentic..150
Be lit...150
Sudden splash..150
Caringly..150
To wed you...151
Gracious smile..151
Intend to stay 152
Their heart..152
Togetherness..152
Trust me..152
Awaken...153
Infiltrate...153
Don't wait..153
Serve us..153
Compensate...154
All have...154
Harmony...154
Put aside...154
Clear to see..155
Unstable..155
Rustles..155
What's right?..155
Giving love..156
Row by row...156
Stormy weather..156
Row by row...156
Overdrive..156
Row by row...156

XXXIX

Peace within

Peace within

Neighboring children..158
Shared..158
Mission...158
Reassures..158
In the morn..159
Vibrant...159
Replenishes..159
Creatures..159
Take flight...160
So free...160
Refreshing strength...160
Like therapy..160
True harmony..161
Always rise..161
To meditate..161
True giver..161
Fragrance...162
As natures do..162
Serenade...162
Really relish..163
Grandeur..163
Tree of life..163
Best treat..163
Clean water..164
Staying alive..164
Endless...164
Vibrant and strong..164
Proudly glitters..165
Bonus luggage...165
Reggae music..165
Love team..165
School days...166
Embrace...167
Authentically pure...167
Yearning for..167
The warmth..167
Dedicated intent...168
Natural muse..168
Songs diversify..168
New season..168
Caribbean Host..169
Sea-side..169
Sandy shores..169
Lifetime..169

XLI

Peace within

Warning sign...170
In reality..170
Kindness..170
My brow..170
Vitamin D...171
By example...171
Lesson of love..171
Greatness..171
Natural purity...172
Devotion...172
Amplify..172
Peace within...172
Essentially..173
Don't rattle...173
Our time...173
Detaches...173
Bits and peices...174
Useful stand...174
Groundwork...174
Activate..174

XLII

XLIII

The loving touch

XLIV

The loving touch

Greater	176
Lifetime	176
Truly grand	176
Needy brew	176
Finally see	177
Attribute	177
These gems	177
Your quest	177
Real dedication	178
Receive	178
Elevate	178
Required	178
Determine stride	179
Shall surpass	179
Guide	179
Skills	179
Justly request	180
Key	180
Succeed	180
Achieve	180
She enlighten	181
Can grow	181
Message	181
Mission	181
A winner	182
True light	182
Renewal	182
Inspired	182
Genuine	183
Shares	183
Endure	183
Gratitude	183
Content	184
Vital	184
Persist	184
Choices	184
Nothing new	185
Fulfilled	185
Endeavor	185
Efficient	185
Her natural	186
Foundational	186
Sacrificing	186

The loving touch

Devotion..186
Dreams..187
Can lead...187
Bright...187
Strength..187
Wholesomeness..188
Sunshine...188
Abode...188
Substance...188
Your means..189
Insatiable..189
Straighten...189
Regular...189
Ambition..190
Fortitude..190
Awareness..190
Strongest..190
Journey...191
Aspire...191
Kind heart..191
Focus..191
I'll remember...192
Giving..192
Caring..192
Empathy...192
Thoughtfulness..193
Igniting..193
Kindness..193
Openness..193
Giant lift..194
True love...194
Healthier..194
Beautiful..194
Our teacher..195
All students...195
Knowledge..195
Conclusion..195
To respond..196
Our journey...196
Guidance...196
Open heart..196
Rosa Parks..197
Courage...197

The loving touch

Open sea shore..198
Ginger beer..198
Sea grape tree..198
Unify..198
Truly essential...199
Elevating...199
Beautiful hillside...199
Evermore...199
These attributes...200
Morality...200
Grace..200
Balance..200
Favorite flower..201
Loving human...201
Divine state...201
Honesty...201
And now it's my turn..202

Confidence and desire

Confidence
Our struggles will teach us how to grow right now
It has all the wisdom that is needed to truly become
As we learn, confidence will set the root to endow
In the right places that we'll have a better outcome

Aspire
Going beyond to achieve our desire and to arrive
We've earned the stamina that's needed to strive
Always searching for definiteness to really aspire
Finishing the entire chore we've started as require

Our midst
In our midst there will be those that back bite us
Thinking they are getting an easy ride to the end
Yet we know they are slipping without a bonus
When they deceive our trust and strictly pretend

Can succeed
We have to remind our self that we can succeed
Before our will power decide to get up and recede

Be done

Even though it's not easy, it can be done
Gathering needed parts while on the run
Life puts us through difficulties every day
Then leave us to find our wandering way

The seeker

Look around us you can see ever so clear
That we all needed help in our career
Nothing ever comes easy for the seeker
Yet that doesn't give a pass to be weaker

Next move

It's not a crime to ponder your next move
Please don't wait for friends to approve
Finishing what you've started is the solution
To all of our uninvited worthless intrusion

Drifting

We should never for a moment, fall asleep
Drifting down the ravine can be very steep

Strength
You're obtainable dream is alive and well
Just give it a kick start with all your might
You'll see how quickly your strength rebel
As you finish a bit at a time, it'll be insight

End result
You can always get away from the screech
That saturate the clarity that you truly need
Thinking of the end result, you will reach
Only a matter of time before you'll succeed

Desire
Though some people will try to disengage
You're desire in many ways than one
Remember you got to increase your wage
Making life more pleasant with lots of fun

Keep on trying
Our location will say not to keep on trying
But it's your liberty you would be denying

Liberation
To believe is the road to our journeys liberation
No matter the struggles we're all going through
We can gain whatever we need in our situation
If we're giving full steadiness in what we pursue

Trueness
When remembering the pure taste of true success
It will put us on the path with elevating trueness
Our thoughts can guide us to real decisive action
When we focus on one thing without distraction

To gain
With seven hours of sleep, we will be ready again
Then we must finish our chores that is in motion
In order to receive all the things we set out to gain
Life will guide us with a steady flow of devotion

A sparkle
A brighter day always bring a sparkle that release
Our endeavor that has the power and lasting peace

Persisting
There is a fortune to be made in most misfortunes
We have to see the real substance inside the game
Most cases persisting with different types of tunes
Until we find the answers in the sturdy mainframe

In due time
Be ready for your plans to progress into real deed
When you give it the fire that it is needed to roar
It will explode; in the trend you have plant the seed
In due time, life will show you how to really soar

Your duty
Most people won't point out the road to liberation
It is your duty to see the signs along your flight
That will bring you all that is in your imagination
With great attraction bursting to do what is right

Make me realize
So-call friends saying one thing yet will deceive
Makes me realize our task must now be achieve

Steady future
Making real sacrifices to go beyond
Is what we need for a steady future?
Thinking only will never correspond
With our keenness and gifted nature

Elevating
It's a great idea elevating a friend
Making sure to take their advice too
No time should be wasted to ascend
Where you can shine with a new crew

Your want
Jealous people will destroy your want
Not caring of the blight they'll spread
All they see is what they always want
With a protective mind situate to shred

Our dream
Our duty is to protect our vibrant esteem
Going the extreme to stick with our dream

Genuine aspiration
Starting over from a lone measly scratch
You're genuine aspiration will be hatch
It will take many tries before you'll win
That's why there's no room for giving in

Our upkeep
We all have to earn all that we keep
Getting it free, always weaken our upkeep
You may say now, that you will take it all
Remember though, of the sleeping pitfall

Inner core
Never scorn a person who kept on trying
Success must listen without ever defying
I know you have tried many times before
Though the answer is in your inner core

Complete
The beauty of life you can truly complete
When you give, until all weakness retreat

Newness
Whatever you do, always leave room to grow
Never fall asleep in your peruse of newness
Getting comfortable can destroy you're glow
Slowing you down in every way that express

Detour
A job for life no longer a common thinking
We have to create a sustenance that endure
If we are to eliminate this gradual sinking
We must turn off that road and take a detour

Arise
Life wasn't meant to be a follower forever
Paving our own way is the ultimate prize
Never mind who's trying to act truly clever
It's your birth right to command and arise

Humbleness
A wonderful feeling to speak what's inside
Then live, with the most humbleness stride

Will change
Use your free time more effectively
Then your whole life will change
Wasting time can get unproductively
If you're routine is not pre-arrange

To bestowed
Working all week for the stingy boss
Might pay some of what we owed
Now procrastination must be toss
Leaving real room only to bestowed

Break the spell
We can pretend that all is well
Or take a useful chance somehow
I believe it's time to break the spell
With the little time that's been allow

Get out
At times we can hardly get out of bed
Yet if we don't, life will be more dread

Were perfect
If a person's life were perfect then there wouldn't be anything to write about. Love stories would not exist; painful relationship wouldn't be talk about.

A moment
Stop and think for a moment, if your life were perfect there wouldn't be an adventure. Poets from years gone by, has left us with some very good foundation.

Ease your mind
In any situation a poet will come to mind, and then you shall remember how a few subtle words do ease your mind.

Share
Most poets never become famous until they are dead, but I'm sure they didn't write for fame, they just want to share the wisdom they carry around in their head.

Daffodil
I'll be going now, have to be with the daffodil that grows beyond the gully and across the rolling hills.

Natural
Natural beings isn't running wild
They are hard to come by, yet always in style

Pure and true
Regular creatures are pure and true
Now without them what would we do?
We need them in times of disappointment
Knowing they will bring some improvement

Guidance

Guidance they will suggest if we'll let them in
Real beings won't cause any damage
Because they know when you hurt another, it's all-in vain

Stride

It's time we recognize that honest people are on our side
Giving us their all in every stride

Precious love

Where there's no bonding, there can be no responding. If our children separated from us just for a little bit, precious love we hold dearly became like a counterfeit. Bonding start at a very young age, if we lose sight of that, their memories will be in a permanent cage.

Time

As time goes by we'll be saying, we should have done this or that, but all should have, can never mend the loose connection.
Most of us must pay a heavy price; as time eats up the wishes and hope we have set aside. We're sure life didn't start out this way, sometime our sorrows waited for us and together our sacred love permanently decayed.

Gentleness

Woman of mutual kindness, stay close to me for with you I've got to share my unconditional gentleness. When uncertainties stick around, you showed me that you'd always be around

Sweetest love

Keep your splendor close at hand; never will I stray for one second. True love is hard to come by, then I won't waste time telling lies. Dearest lover of all loveliness, you're sweetest love I must digest. Woman with love so true, how can we ever be blue.

New conclusion

When you're tired and have no solution
Leave the door open for the next day
You'll be amaze of the new conclusion
That will put you promptly on your way

Strength

Your strength will come back together
If you remember what life has to give?
Doesn't matter if you're under the weather
Now is the time to clearly be progressive

Make amend

When we try to reach out a little bit more
The loose ends will tighten up at the end
Time to show all discarded ideas the door
Then make amend with a doing type friend

Ultimate

From now on, when things seems unsure
I will know where to find the ultimate cure

Enough time
Look beyond to acquire your dreams
Enough time has been wasted already
Procrastinating for too long it seems
Now everything needed to be steady

Have to
Have to move more aggressively
To set the move into real action
The days of crawling passively
Has gone with a lowly distraction

Objective
Today I must carry out my objective
That will guide me to the real source
Too often I have been too selective
 That is why I've thrown off course?

Whole heart
Have to put my whole heart into gear
Before the end of a misgiving year

Make a start
It's good when we can make a start
In the direction where we want to go
Remembering to be very, very smart
As we might have to travel solo

Gooder
Life could be gooder as we choose
If we plan to really follow through
Don't fall asleep and take a snooze
You're chances will become a few

Goodest
To believe is the goodest attribute
It gives the foundation to our dream
Then make it possible to contribute
In the world to the highest extreme

When
When we lose our drive to become
Spank it, till we get a better outcome

For you
Got to push for you, even when no one believe in you
You don't need permission to secure what you desire
If your desire is strong and willing to push on through
It will find a way to search and ignite the sleeping fire

Misgiving
Who said it was easy starting a new way of true living
Sometimes we're surrounded by doubters at our location
But remember who will be dealing with the misgiving
When we ignore our doing, in this abrasive situation

Durability
Now I've learn the ins and outs of everyday durability
I will make sure, not to make the same mistake again
Paying attention will enhance my lesson in prosperity
Following through is the vehicle to profit and true gain

Truly sublime
Belief is the strongest word that exist in our life time
Giving us the power to create whatever is truly sublime

Watch as much

You can watch as much as you want
But that won't change anything at all
Wasting time is a virus you've plant
This gives powers that make us stall?

Listen

You can listen wherever you now go
Without a plan, it is hard to expand
Life will never change for tomorrow
If our circumstance is like contraband

Until

You can talk until you are no more
Your situation will always be the same
Pretending is never a reliable cure
It really messes up you're good name

Doing

Only by doing the act of the task
Can we receive the life that we've ask

Two steps

Always be two steps in front of your quest
Watch it with every breath you breathe
Never waver in your decision you've invest
See it through in whatever work conceive

Our duty

We can get tired on our off days sometime
As our strength will be a little out of tune
It's our duty to stay focus in the meantime
With what we have desire before it is ruin

Use of time

Time won't be too gracious later on in life
It will be in short supply as our years go by
Got to make use of time and fight the strife
That way, our search won't be disqualify

Awake

A zigzag tunnel in every journey we take
Yet we'll have to keep our purpose awake

Learning how

Time can only get better from here
All the doubt will fall by the wayside
Learning how to face the new frontier
Experience is the teacher and a guide

Pursue

Forsaking the things you shouldn't do
Will give strength to your real cause
Now you can focus on what to pursue
Without hinder or pointless applause

Enlighten

I'm already shifted in the strongest gear
To reach my ultimate way of living
My vision is truly more than clear
In the new world of enlighten living

Stay away

Will stay away from those who slander
Don't want to repeat worthless blunder

On course

Whatever is worthwhile is never easy
Surprises will throw you off course
Re-setting your sails when it's breezy
You'll find your way back on course

It's time

When we need answers right away
It often elude us without caution
No matter the sinking feeling today
It's time to put our boots into action

Refresh

Have to refresh our mind everyday
About the things that keep us going
Not wise to get lost and go astray
In the undertaking that we're doing

Be employ

Sticking to our vision that we enjoy
We can find the tools to be employ

Make it

It's up to you to make it happen right now
Waiting can only put a splinter in your dream
Have to get going, regaining our life somehow
Not so wise depending on some lucky scheme

Why wait

As long as you have strength, use it all the way
Why wait and then complain in your later year
That all of your vibrant power has gone away
There's no perfect start in life, so get into gear

Overdue

You will never know what you're friends can do
Until they have concluded their lifetime mission
Why sit on a fence, your success is well overdue
It's clear to see you no longer need permission

Satisfaction

Taking charge of your own life, is a real blessing
It gives you the satisfaction that's truly missing

True desire
I must reignite my true desire
To pursue all that I embrace
Time is moving down to the wire
Now we got to change our work place

New strategies
No time to feel sorry for our living
We have to turn this hinder on its head
Then re-focus on new strategies of giving
All that we can, towards our life instead

Objective
Some days when we feel truly lost
We have to rest our ongoing weariness
Then tackle our real objective at all cost
Regardless of all the blistered tiredness

Revisit
We have to revisit our dream right now
No matter the sweat that falls from our brow

Coax it back

When hardship has dissected your will to do
Remember your inner strength never departed
Coax it back into the route where it's overdue
Only have to strengthen the road that's charted

Today's living

There is no easy street in today's living
We all have to live within our daily struggle
Doing what we can, we're hardly surviving
Yet we have to regain our resolve to juggle

Sunshine

Paying part of each bills that we can now
Then wait for the mail to see who is in line
Remember you will get through this somehow
At the end of every adversity there's sunshine

Test of time

We all have to go through the test of time
In order to amass what is ours in our lifetime

Existence

When your existence is at a sticky end
Think of compromise in what you do
The time has come when you can't pretend
That our tattered being shouldn't be review

Ideas

Entangled with continuous disappointment
Is never a good thing to really cherish?
Always be looking for ideas to implement
Or at the end of the day we all will perish

Adjust

Luckily there is a new road we can take
Treating each other with respect and trust
In no time, can we ever truly be awake
If we don't give reasonable room to adjust

A balance

When there is a balance in what we're doing
We'll come full circle in what we're pursuing

Transpire
Knock unto the door of your desire
There it will start to grow into being
Feel your inner strength transpire
In all that exists in your trying being

Achieve
Seek ways to achieve what's needed
Then you will be in the right place
Get what's needed before it receded
Beyond your grasp without a trace

Take the time
We can find what is require in life
If we now take the time to reel it in
Nothing comes easy without the strife
We know that, in our daily searching

Lofty living
To believe in our desire all the way
Is the real secret to lofty living today?

Induce

Today I refuse to be confused
The unexpected won't do me in
My willpower I will induce
With all my might from within

Already wired

Even though I'm truly tired
Soon my desire must come true
A mission to do, I'm already wired
Have to remember in everything I do

Half way

Life test all who require a better life
Never letting go, till you prove it all
Half way is really a recipe for strife
It cannot hear someone's flimsy call

You're duty

Some days can appear so pointless
But its you're duty to demand success

An aim
Courage likes to play a waiting game
It waits for you to make up your mind
Then will follow if you have an aim
That won't waste time or lazily resigned

My life
Could never reside to wait for a person
Whose main objective is to mislead?
My life would in every way be worsen
With no intention to do a real good deed

Way out
Despite what we may face in life today
We got to look at the best way out
No time should be wasted everyday
With things we can't do anything about

Our will
Every problem that tries to ambush our will
Must be shown the door without a tainted refill

Liberating
Need to acquire my full strength again
Too many break messes up everything
Full time to reach for a liberating gain
That will cease me from my wobbling

Perfect time
Got to remind myself what's needed?
When my mind wanders off my work
Not right to fret over what's depleted
Now is the perfect time to network

Fulfillment
Can see time is moving very swiftly
While my fulfillment is slowing down
Have to edge in my doing significantly
Before time chases me out of the town

Readiness
I must reunite with my readiness to pursue
All that is willing with a new clear avenue

Small steps
Should get rid of the unwanted clutter now
It will remove the hindrance that devastate
Many things need to be lighten somehow
Taking small steps is the way to delegate

Life of peace
Wasted belief, love to house a big fight
Making sure we believe in every smear
Today is the right time to show it the light
Returning to a life of peace without despair

Renew
Our minds like to play tricks as we endure
With foolish repetition that really subdue
Always have to make clear then reassure
The life that we seek will be truly renew

Stand firm
We got to stand firm with a new desire
If we want the new life that we so require

Perseverance
We need to have a sturdy balance
Whatever we're going to pursue
That will ensure perseverance
In all things we are planning to do

On course
Turning to an awaiting force
We can change what is needed
When our focus is on course
Life lessons always succeeded

To achieve
We all have some hesitation
About what we are to achieve
One way to a new position
Applying what you've conceive

Antidote
You can really keep a tight note
Knowing you've got the antidote

Biggest advertiser
Word of mouth is the biggest advertiser
Then why not let it be the great equalizer
Tell your friends about this energy poetry
It can transform them, with the right entry

Fruitful society
Where the purpose of the message is just
We don't have to pretend with disgust
Giving a helping hand is always the key
To a more fruitful society we'll ever see

Progress
I do believe the time is just right to give
To others so they can progress and live
In a world that cares for every existence
Spreading kindness we'll go the distance

Pure love
Can you imagine a world with pure love?
Where we no longer have to push and shove

Wake up

Don't spend money you don't possess
It's time to wake up and exit this mess
Creating a budget is the only way out
Never mind who's taking the old route

Uplifted

Approaching with a brand new thinking
Now you are uplifted instead of sinking
A fresh idea can put you in front today
Instead of waiting, to go on your way

Complete

Keep in mind your dream to complete
I know when you do, it will be so sweet
Can see that beautiful smile from here
All that we've talked about is now clear

Guidance

From now on, you know I'll be around
With real guidance that's truly profound

Your strength
Got to make the most of time right now
Or it will truly make the most of you
Why waste your strength anyhow
With these doubts you have outgrew

Lighthouse
We all know that time is a moving thing
It has no friends in a redundant house
Waiting for the ideal move, will sting
Time to get a view from the lighthouse

What's overdue?
Real wisdom can be shared as require
We can always learn what to truly do
Cultivated our chances to really aspire
Got to push the fire on what's overdue

Success
Our energy we should never suppress
Time to bring home our needed success

See the idea
We all learn something new every single day
Take time to see the idea within the meaning
Not wise to let the secret of life go a stray
When we could uplift our life from learning

Get moving
Can get moving in the right way we intend
If we put more energy into our affirmation
It won't be easy breaking the very old trend
Yet it is time to invite a modern situation

Beyond
At times we've gotten these strange feeling
Of what we are suppose to do right now
Not clever to put off the action for healing
Have to forge beyond our pain somehow

A price
What we ask for, always come with a price
Be prepared to give your all, take my advice

Another person

Why put all your energy in another person quest
After it's over, they will pass you with no regret
Demanding is the tradition of their full conquest
Excluding you is very easy after you have sweat

Full time

Its full time you start thinking about your target
Shaping it into life before you are unsteadily old
There will always be some need for that market
That you are withholding from the threshold

Bits and pieces

Your drive will come in bits and pieces each day
And it is your obligation to enforce its calling
Most people won't go out of their way to convey
What you should be doing or really overhauling

Your move

It is your move, to do what's now best for you
Don't wait for a lifetime deciding on what to do

Wake you up
Walking in another person's shoe
Will wake you up to what is genuine
Reminding you of what life can do
When you have an actual deadline

Definite solution
The rent can drain most of your power
Make you think of a definite solution
Regaining your strength by the hour
Facing a new day with real attribution

Until we see
Sometimes we think life is unbearable
Until we see our neighbors problem
Working on small difficulty is curable
We only have to try and solve them

Doing
With a little bit of doing each day
Our task will reduce and finally decay

Precision

Little things keep the world from sinking
It helps the inhabitants in their mission
Love is the ruler of all resolute thinking
Guiding who want to win with precision

Key message

Soon we must use our new key message
To carry out our own purpose tomorrow
Teaching can help us to gain our passage
When we show our student what we know

Self-confidence

Leading by example can give real power
To those who need that extra influence?
Their search will never get boring or sour
The only thing awaits is self-confidence

Solution

Honesty and trust is a vital conclusion
Mastering small ideas into real solution

Determination
For everyone whose really trying
You're relentless desire will be there
When you're strength seems to be dying
Determination will show you how to care

Dedication
Success is not an accident in the waiting
It's all in the planning and real dedication
We will put in the work then contemplating
Which is the greatest recommendation?

Persistence
Nothing can ever replace a constant deed
It grinds procrastination out of existence
Making success deliberately guaranteed
With your immense quality of persistence

You're gate
No reason to create excuses then hesitate
Whatever you need, is right at you're gate

Take control
Renew your tired brain and release the strain
Why dwell on wasteful thoughts that constrain
Now is the time to take control of your source
With the bits and pieces you can be on course

Understand
Don't give much thought to those who slander
Watch them from a distance like a bystander
You should put your energy to a useful stand
One that have a plan that you can understand

Don't hesitate
Most days you will be drain being over-work
Nothing will change without the groundwork
That's when you must start to think of you
Don't hesitate to practice what you should do

Activate
You must be the first to activate your desire
Then you will receive what you have enquire

Never mind
Never mind the relapse here and there
Everyone will earn their needed lesson
To be successful in what we truly care
Setting sails again without the guessing

Life will
It's not right to fall through the crack
There is no time to be wasting time
Life will always keep you on track
When you're willing to work overtime

To believe
Turning up the real heat, is to believe
That your resolve must be in overdrive
To bring forth what you have conceive
Is the most satisfactory way to strive?

Start over
Don't ever forget to start over again
When difficulties mess with your brain

Satisfied
Resistance always gives into real persistence
Doesn't matter how many times you've tried
Leaving the company of negative assurance
Always the best thing to make you satisfied?

Worthwhile
When you are out of energy, just rest a bit
New ideas will be on your side in a while
To lead you out of all hurtful desire to quit
Staying the course will make it worthwhile

Diamond platter
Most people won't receive a free flight
On a diamond platter at their front door
They must try with their earnest might
Every chance they find to really explore

No one
No one cares how many times you've fallen
It's your duty to rise to your chosen calling

To win
Accept change, if you want your life to change
Only you can induce your imagination to win
In the direction that you have plan to arrange
Then you're responsiveness can really begin

Above defeat
We are all timid when it comes to a new goal
But that's what makes the victory so sweet
It's more than refreshing, being in control
Of our lives, if we are to rise above defeat

Readiness
Getting comfortable can bind us to tardiness
With no chance of ever breaking lose soon
We will have to establish a vibrant readiness
To elevate our dream that we have attune

Obstacles
As we face the constant obstacles everyday
Must remember the cause and be on our way

Our thoughts

Awareness is a miracle substance that gives fortitude
It delivers what we have been devotedly seeking
Guiding our thoughts to a truly essential clear attitude
Where we can start with anew for what we're seeking

A flicker

Insights can quench the nervousness in our exploring
Only need a flicker of truth to put us on the route
That will carry us through way beyond our scoring
Leaving no room for laziness to hurt us throughout

Real handle

Understanding, that's where you have the real handle
From that angle you can steer the ship in any direction
Life will unfold all the things that you have mishandle
Then put you back in the saddle to make all correction

Consciousness

Consciousness clears the mind and heart in whatever
That we can truly undertake, making us more clever

Impress

You have come too close to give up anyhow
Remember you have to face the test of success
Before you can enjoy the fruit you have endow
Your belief and resolute must be totally impress

Ambush

Keep your mind on the outcome of your plan
Many people will try to ambush your dream
While reaping the rewards like a middleman
With watchers, fighting you to the extreme

Golden spoon

Don't wait for a golden spoon to be given
Preparation is your ultimate way to liberation
Finish all the vocation that makes you driven
Never give in despite how tough the situation

Graceful

After giving so many years of your time
Your prizes will be well graceful and prime

Prosperous
We all suffer from sadness in some dreadful way
But that doesn't mean we should embrace idleness
When our life is nudging away from hardship today
Take your chances to a new and prosperous address

Positive shift
We all feel beaten at some point in this open ocean
 Remembering though we must gather the real potion
 In order to fulfill our life destiny with realistic worth
Got to move one limb, with a positive shift to unearth

Chances
Every one of us will face hardship in our lifetime
Yet how could we sit down while our chances fade
No matter who said what, life will make you climb
In every way that you intend to give and persuade

Concise
Being concise is a secret that everyone has truly learn
Then why not get to the point, so we can now discern

Renewal
The quietness and tiredness in our life today
Will really show us what is on our fragile mind
Never mind who doesn't want to go out and play
A true sense of genuine renewal we've got to find

Silent killer
Being exhausted from work is a silent killer of time
It wears you out, then cuts you down in your prime
All those who want to embrace real consciousness
Have to plough deep into nature to find its trueness

Solitude
I'm eager to find the solitude that I need to endure
To get away from the abrasive task of my course
I need to be revived fiscally and mentally to ensure
To face tomorrows demand that is always on course

Essential
Essential it is, that I must sort out my direction today
To relieve all the unwanted strings from my doorway

Our 2008 Jamaican Olympians W.I "The world fastest"

There was no real contest
We are the world fastest
Usain is our bolt of lighting
Blazing the meters and sprint
Before we could even blink
The medals was easy picking

Really, you know what
The 2008 Olympic is where it's at
Our men and women are the best
A lot faster than all the rest
Gold, silver and bronze
We gotten it all from our icons

Megastar Shelly-Ann Fraser
Was much sharper than a laser
Simpson daring Sherone
Push on with all her heart
Kerron fearless Stewart
Fight it down to the bone

Walker superstar Melaine
Crush the opposition down the lane
Our great Asafa Powell
With all the champion maker
No other team was greater
Cause Nesta Carter was a real duel

Rosemarie sensational Whyte
Never gives up without a fight
Shereefa amazing Lloyd
And Williams fiery Novelene
Together With Bobby- Gaye wilkings
They are our lean mean machines?
Shericka Williams is so amplified
Veronica gifted Campbell Brown
Runs the competition to the ground

Genuine

Why sit back and be used without a fight
You may need a push to restart your desire
When that moment appear with a dim light
Get moving with a genuine purpose to aspire

New avenue

Though my struggle have been hard and long
I know that I must be determined and strong
If you allow pushers of paper to control you
Then there is no real chance for a new avenue

Alert

Always be on the alert for that radiant flash
Regardless how deep you are in a nose dive
Only you can really avert the awaiting crash
That users of the world has set up to deprive

Wiser

Remember, you are wiser than days gone by
Now is the perfect time to start then multiply

Greater

You should make your day greater anyway
When there's so much hardship that lingers
Remember that difficulties in life never stay
It always gets tired and withdrawn their stingers

Persuasion

Create the result that is in your active imagination
With real dedication and lasting lively persuasion
Continue to push on with your aim in full force
When you are resolve, how can you be off course?

Doable passage

Waiting for a great event to take place is not wise
Little by little you have to crunch the doable passage
Even when life seems so rough, success will arise
Now by the lake, you'll enjoy your beautiful cottage

Fruition

Whatever we want out of life, we got to believe
In order for it to matured into fruition and achieve

Bounce back

When the sadness of life is lifted, a plan of action must be listed
We have to push our will to reclaim all the inner force we need
In order to bounce back from those obstacles that was enlisted
We must see the whole picture from different angles to succeed

Fresh outlook

With a fresh outlook on life we can gather the energy we require
Ignite the fire from deep within our rested souls and eager desire
The time is now that we must finish what we have brag about
Driving home the rock that all ideas is needed to end the drought

First glow

Nothing will happen without that first glow that we all have inside
Got to coax it out of its resting place then set it ablaze with action
Never mind if you are a bit anxious, your act will let it all subside
Now, bringing home the prize is the name of the whole transaction

Your policy

Don't be distracted by someone's greed and never-ending craving
Stick to your policy that you have created with your own engraving

Unity
Finding the truth in what you do
Then liberation will be yours to keep
Unity will give strength to the crew
It operates better when life gets steep

Devotion
The missing pieces that we now require
Will come together with actual devotion
That is waiting to transform our desire
Into real skills and permanent solution

Will grow
Power is always honest togetherness
That has no hidden mask to separate
The foundation of our united progress
Will grow stronger as we participate

Sacred
Whatever we invite in our life today
Must be affirmative in every sacred way

Consistence

Never surrender your search for a better existence
Regardless of the difficulties they try to introduce
Now it depends on your desire to be consistence
With what you have set forth in motion to produce

The reason

Watch not the idle ones that is so easily slow to act
To gain what you truly want, don't give all that slack
When you're low on the energy to push on forward
Remember the reason of your quest, to stir onward

Explore

If we would only exercise the wisdom we have today
We will get whatever we set out to achieve and more
A free lunch won't be around the corner everyday
Then why not go all out with your ideas and explore

Give

The greatest feeling is to finish what we have started
It give the tools that is needed in the sea we've charted

The leader
The leader, who leads with love, will have no problem with their followers of the blessed land. Conflict will cease to exist; when people refuse to use their fist.

Real power
Love is the only real power, if you are traveling on a self-indulgence road, then you will end up under the broken tower.

Honesty
Most leaders of today speak of honesty, but they only use it as a part of their vocabulary. When leading by example, what then can enter such wholesome rudder?

Act of love
Most of the world is puzzled by the simple act of love, yet it conquered all unwanted cruelty and then gives a beautiful flower of everlasting life.

Selected dream
I've got to keep this inner push from slipping
It tends to get lazy when I ease off my selected dream

Realizing
Realizing that I'm the captain of my ship
Can't give command to just anyone, cause they might slip

Avenues

Willing to get going then goes into neutral
Won't benefit anyone whatsoever
We've got to push on even when our chances seems slim
Keeping all avenues open to the very end

Stamina

Some-time confusion will gobble up our stamina
But we must remember the reason why we're on our quest
This inner push has invited itself in
Now let the steam pour progressively from within

Revive

Give your heart a bit more time to regroup
Then the answers will come back to you
Don't try to rush what you're trying recoup
Time will revive all what you're trying to do

Out of exile

When you think of the things you want in life
They have a tendency to appear after awhile
It's you duty to take your mind off the strife
Allowing the new life to spring out of exile

Steadily

Your mind can be your best friend everyday
If you let it travel in a steadily clear manner
Tightening the loose ends in the passageway
You can now become the number one planner

Recuperate

Everyone needs a real moment to recuperate
From the everyday thinking that confiscate

Laugher is free
Laughter is free medicine for our tired heart and mind
Taking it whenever you are stressed out at home or work
No need to spend money that is in short supply to unwind
It makes a world of difference when life is not a patchwork

Not in a bottle
The cure for sadness is not in a bottle that is very expensive
Feel the honesty that pores freely from your daily extensive
All things that are real, needs nothing to hold it together
Nature will heal itself with the needed stuff that's healthier

Dependable
When the hardship of life tries to pressure your well being
Take a walk and replenish your tired soul that needs a break
Can easily lose sight of our plans when we are not overseeing
We need to be dependable, with all things and staying awake

Happiness
When we invite happiness in, we won't need so much expertise
Rejuvenation of our soul will prevent all kind of useless disease

Your will
Never give up your dream no matter how hard it seem
Your will won't walk away, when you activate its drive
No time should be wasted on promises of an empty regime
That has no intension to give heartily, but only to deprive

Essence to build
Staying power has the essence to build our golden spoon
While life awaits to see if we are creditable of the freight
What we have so eagerly demand from the opportune
We must give every ounce of wisdom in order to cultivate

Ultimate prize
While friends having all the so-call fun on the weekend
We must grind it out, to hone in on the ultimate prize
Time will find us where we are and deliver its dividend
When we consciously open our mind to act plus organize

Create and achieve
We must turn up our burning desire to give then receive
Then and only then, will we be able to create and achieve

Determination

The doer
Persistence is self power
It separates the watcher from the doer

Can inflict
Many interruptions will persist
But remember what indecision can inflict

Furlong
Pause not for too long
You might not be able to go on to the extra furlong

Your side
When momentum is on your side
Keep the flames going because it will slide?

Given gift
As doubt tries to drag you under
It is you're given gift to get stronger

Golden spoon
Sticking to a real foundation
It will bring true revelation
Remember most people didn't receive a golden spoon
Now's a good time to take action before you're ideas are completely ruined

How long
Doesn't matter how long you've been out of
Commission
Don't ever give up your inspirational vision

Has to pay
Build the foundation and the roof won't be far behind
I've been ripped off too, one has to pay to learn, and that's the only way you'll earn your keep

Into place

Now you must go on your way and rise above this slight
set back, time won't beg you to come along, so stick
with whatever is your calling, in due time everything
will fall into place.

Humble giving

Maintaining the wings that fly's, Guarantees life
mission before we die. Humble giving is a brilliant
thing; it keeps our wants in tune with everything.

Be kept

Sitting here in front of a bird cleaning its feathers, a
flash of inspiration I've gathered. In order to keep our
resilient strong; it has to be kept in mint condition.

Ride the waves

Make up your mind in whatever you really want to do
Jumping from one thing to another won't bring us success
Ride the waves no matter how tall they may be
Very soon these uncertainties will flee

Times of need

Most friends won't come to your rescue in times of need
Even though you have much mouth to feed
When you're truly dedicated taking care of other people's monies
Just remember your true potential is really at stake

Validate

Consistency can work wonders
Then take the time to ponder what you're under
Look at all that energy we put into other people's empire
Then at age forty we are no longer for hire
It's a good feeling when navigating your own ship
We only have to stay the course to validate our leadership

Inside
Poetry from within can ignite a new beginning
Seek deeply inside our soul and we'll find what makes us tick

Time to teach
Seeing beyond our reach, we must take the time to teach Poetry's intention is to share with all creatures of the universe to make their world a better place. If we didn't brag and boast about who has the most, we would be serving at a different and natural post.

Cross road
Can't wait forever, I'm sitting here at the cross road and don't know which train to board. Nothing ever comes easy; when we are off balance. Not getting younger and the days are much shorter. It's time to take these hesitant steps. Starting out is always simple but finishing up take a lot more work.

Take a stand
Thoughts of confusion will be close at hand, but now I've got to remember to take a stand. Nodding off to sleep won't help the situation, time to put into place greater expectation.

Such a test
Won't be rushing off to some make- shift tent, we must give this unwanted struggle a huge dent. Often we've wondered off in distress, and then wonder why life has to be such a test. Without authentic dedication, reality will never manifest into the life we all dream about.

Adapt
Don't be afraid of changes
Which are bound to happen?
Don't fight it, just learn to adapt
But that doesn't mean you should take unwanted crap

Face the facts
No need to hide around the corner
Face the facts or you'll be a goner
It's ok to be nervous
Remember not to make unnecessary fuss

Just delayed
Sometime changes make you grow up
Maturity won't stir until truth start to erupt
Why lie down and cry when things don't go your way
Changes are imminent some time they're just delayed

Sitting here
Sitting here waiting for the right thing to happen is a soggy way of life. Time will catch up to you, so it's best to push on through before life change its route.

Own future
We want to do what we want but familiar grounds won't let go. Criticism from someone close at times will delay your spunk of the go get it attitude, however don't throw away your aim to get cracking. There are those who will tell you it's ok to relax and life will take care of the matter. Now you would be fooling yourself, if you were not in control of your own future.

Comforting
Familiar grounds are ever so comforting and easygoing; the tragedy of too much sleep is that some of us never wake up to tell the story, the story of the inner pain and frustration that laziness brings to the heart and soul of our lives.

Look beyond
Grappling with this win some, lose some scenario, we only have to look beyond our feet. The time has come to go forth with our activities, now that we have a definite clue.

Lump sum
Signs of life approach in small proportion; you only have to mix it with revelation. The how will be revealed, but only if we stay the course. Win some; lose some, not all that is acquired come in a lump sum.

Inside my heart
Courage and understanding must be encouraged if we are to reach our destination. When your nerves become weak and the future looks bleak, remember others are much weaker than you are. Some will go to bed without food tonight, and deep down inside my heart, I feel their sorrow and despair.

Duty
We, who have the strength and the know-how, please don't stand idle and watch. When you mix courage with duty, won't be long before you find the right clue. Understanding is one of the greatest champions of survival; it steers us away from adversity when the era gets crucial.

Loosen the knot
Let's not waste time anymore, you've got the key to life then why not open the door. It make no sense criticizing the have not, give them a chance and show them the ropes so they can loosen the knot.

Be thirsty
Be thirsty for everyday knowledge, or your brain will turn to porridge. No need to retreat from today's living and shut the sunlight out of your life. We must use the vibrant energy which is all so powerful, break out of our sorrowful shell and gel.

A start
All we need is a start in what we want and remember to knock down the word can't. It's a muddle to wait for someone to open the door of opportunities while you stand back and watch. If that's the case, be ready to embrace what have been chosen for you without complaint.

Lead thy self
One thing at a time and everything will work out just fine. Soon you'll find out, you don't have to work for nickels and dimes. Lead thy self to the promise land; wait not for others to make you understand. With a solid plan in hand, crank up the engine and don't idle for too long.

Maturity
These vehicles have tendencies to get over heated, if you don't get out of bed. Don't jump from one thing to another before you really understand, or you might pay a heavy price with dollars in hand. Maturity is a good thing; but we always have to wait until it's our turn.

Trials and errors
How do they accomplish their task you may ask, with trials and errors, before they can see the sparks? One thing at a time and everything will work out just fine.

Rise up

Rise up weary seeker, or your days will be bleaker.
Though you are tired and broke, you've got to move forward even with a minimal stroke. Distraction is an everyday menace; we have to remember it's just a nuisance. Once we're sure of where we want to go, let no one shut the open door. Take what's truly yours; fear not of the little hardship you will endure.

Long enough

You can dream big too, waste no time feeling blue. There is so many things you can do, remember the correct key is in you. Stick with your goal long enough and you won't stay in the rough. We need just a taste of success, and then the rest will be the easiest. Dreams are the first step to our ambition, as we'll have to push on regardless of the hinder. You can learn to go forward and earn what you can, instead of knocking on reluctant doors. No could turn into yes, if we would only persist. Dream does come true if we take the time to execute. Grieve not of yesterday, today we have in our grasp the tools to extract the knowledge we so desperately need.

Security

Walk away from the supposed security, because it's only a foolish figment of the imagination. Got to move away from this imprisonment of my soul, for once it's time to take control. Discouragement will show its ugly head, but that's nothing to dread. Keep the fire of doing and you shall reap the fruit of what you're perusing. Some negative voices might try to twist our minds, but remember who's facing the daily confine. The final step is always the hardest; we got to shake loose the jitters and forsake the nervousness. Walking away from a permanent fixture some-time isn't an easy thing to do, but old useless places will never make your life anew. Procrastination do ruin our precious living, it bring us often to the road that has no ending. Take the necessary steps to be, and taste the freedom that is waiting directly.

Venturing out

If we are not persistent with the knowledge we've acquired; it would be of no use just to be inspired. A lot of visionaries have come and gone, because the fire from their innermost went out too soon. Knowledge is a good thing, that's why we've got to be ready to apply it or it won't mean a thing. Venturing out isn't an easy mission, but when we feel the urge, it is the right decision. Sticking around after so many no's, your chances can only grow.

The ladder
We fear, because we choose not to dare. Isn't it time we face the facts of life, until we take to the ladder, nothing will ever happen.

Crave
Some of us pretending we're brave, but it's only attention that we crave. When the curtain goes down and the mask is removed, would be brave heart just disappear.

The remedy
Timidity is not the remedy for longevity, open your mind and heart then you're in the right location for receptiveness.

Go forth
As you go forth destructive forces will try to overpower you, just remember your purpose in what you are pursuing. We must challenge ourselves all the way, before we can see the eternal light at the end.

Have to study
Its lunchtime, I'm trying to read so I can plant a few promising seeds, but other people just kept banging on the car. With the sweat pouring down my face, I've got to remind myself why I have to study in order to reach my destiny.

Trying
Years had gone by and no fruits have ripened yet,
Can't stop trying now though all I would do is face regret.

Can do
When my journey looks bleak, this can-do attitude I'll keep. The foundation of encouragement I've got to embrace, that is the only way I can ever keep up this challenging pace.

Multitudes
A sudden change in course brings multitudes of reaction. Be careful of the people you trust, they might leave you in the dust

Grown up
Easy for grown up to become just like a switch, at the least chance notice they'll give up authentic certainty for a monetary itch.

Deliberate
A sudden rush of inspiration has taken over my way of life. It is time to be deliberate with my occupation, finishing one chore at a time.

Decisive
Inspiration is great when we follow through with decisive action; it teaches us that there is truly a way if we are really determined.

The drive
The drive to do, come every so often, that is the time to put our aspiration in motion. Why not grab a hold of this feeling of inner strength the next time it passes your way.

A new craft
Look in the right direction and you'll find true satisfaction. Sitting up late at night learning a new craft, then tomorrow we can hardly stay awake. The right direction always takes a lot of perspiration and some inspirations.

Stay the course
 In time you'll receive the ultimate crunches, and then free lunches will come in bunches. Stay on course even when only you believe in you, there's no reason to get off track with unwanted issues.

Revisit
People will have to revisit their heart, where true understanding is stored.
So many a fruitless roads we have headed, and still not learning from yesterday's message.

Flow of goals
Facing countless barren ventures and still not watching where we venture. To endure this test of faith, we must look beyond our toes and forward in the direction of truth. Harvesting a flow of goals, then life will take on a new beginning.

Under wraps

Voracity looking candidly in their best suit, but we can see them from afar. Displaying lies that they wear on their ties, as they maintain the have not under wraps. Just one solution to this situation and that is to be in control of your own objective.

Be on hand

Start small then expand, on your way to success land, remember a lot of test will be on hand. Watch out for the beast that lurks within the branches of the forest, they will attack you even before the sun goes down.

Tardiness

Only if I have more time, will be your cry. Laziness will always be looking for more time, waiting for others to do their work.
Because you are always putting off your desire, tardiness will not let you perspire. We all have the same twenty-four hours in one day, but you found it difficult to apply yourself every day.

Sweetness

You must earn your keep, if you want to enjoy the sweetness of life. Only if I have more time, should be a thing of the past, I now believe it's time for you to face your daily task.

Bonus of love
Awareness is the real power that we truly need in our struggling reality
It's at our finger tips, if we so really desire to find our true liberation
When we maintain a steady head towards our aspiration with totality
Life will deliver all that we ask for, with a bonus of love and admiration

Persevere
Why are you only scratching the surface of your wants with apprehension?
When the entire conclusion can truly come true with a bit more persuasion
From a distance watch what the owners do, at your place of employment
Look closely at how they persevere in the undertaking of your deployment

Why wait
Knowing what to do, then doing the necessary work, in time you will see
The result of your labor in many different ways unimagined years to come
You can always start slow then increase your speed as time becomes free
 Why wait for someone to push you to harness your dream to truly become

Worth
The power to know is such a great tool to use at the right moment in time
Dissecting all of the would be problems is of such real worth in a lifetime

Pursue

Poets, don't lose sight of poetry in whatever you do
When life seems to be unfulfilled with obstruction
Crack the code, with new ideas to review and pursue
Only you can change your life with a new invention

Reserve

When our energy is on low with hardly any vital sign
Reach into your reserve, and then follow the guideline
Most days when we are drained with no place to go
Think of your will to carry on and face our tomorrow

Pay our dues

It seems so hard at times to break away from hardship
Yet we must pay our dues in order to reach our dream
We all have to face life ordeal before we can get a grip
Don't pay attention to days that mess up your esteem

Evoke

Just as we feel like throwing in the towel in our day
We must evoke our work that we have greatly display

Greatest

Never give up your dream, no matter how hard it seem
Your will won't walk away, when you activate its fire
With all its ideas that can turn your life to the extreme
Now is the greatest moment to fulfill your just desire

Certain things

To get the edge we always have to finish a bit at a time
Consistently, we can carve out the true figure overtime
When we put in the care that is needed for a great end
We can't leave certain things to our friends to defend

Endow

If we are slow to react to answers that is needed now
We will fall of the stallion before it reaches the line
Embracing the love of what we are trying to endow
Will give us the power to align with the guideline

Unless

Unless we planned to give all of our devotion today
Makes no sense to initiate the flame then go halfway

Fakeish applause

Face the cause before you take a pause
No one will fix your ongoing problem
Don't wait for some fakeish applause
That some proud idea will solve them

Baby steps

Have to take your baby steps right now
Before your strength goes off the edge
Nurse it closely with the aim to endow
Answers you seek is in the knowledge

Faulty Smile

We cannot depend on some faulty smile
That will never pan out in the real end
We need to see which action is hostile
The willful idleness that likes to pretend

Our strength

Have to grab our strength with meaning
Even when it's continuously screaming

Real sequence
Persistence can drive away all sluggish pretence
That tries to interfere with our enduring ambition
As we focus on what we desire in real sequence
We can always acquire it with related action

Advantage
Patience is the gateway to dreams we've create
It gives the nutrition that we so need to activate
Whatever that we will call someday real success
Have to be mould into true advantage to impress

Confidence
Confidence can see us through our biggest snag
No matter how huge the difficulties we now face
Got to reload perseverance with no time to brag
Before it slide and really go off to another place

Believing
Believing is the starting point of every firm dream
It keeps our drive in the right motion that is supreme

Treasure

Reggae girlyz going the extra mile
Playing with sophisticated style
Perseverance they don't lack
Soon they'll be back on the attack
Our soccer team is a true treasure
And watching them is a pleasure

Mystical

Reggae girlyz going the extra mile
With moves that is truly versatile
The chanting of our dedicated fans
Give the players the upper hand
Staying with the mystical rhythm
We know that we will be winning

Grove

Moving the ball within the grove
Our chances is much more sure
Soon we'll have nothing to prove
When our girlyz execute and score

Ingrain

Reggae girlyz going the extra mile
This win will give us a great smile
Soccer we love with all our heart
Playing the game down to an art
Performing their best is ingrain
Capturing the trophy is their aim

Sophisticated

Reggae boyz going the extra mile
Playing with sophisticated style
Perseverance they don't lack
Soon they'll be back on the attack
Our soccer team is a true treasure
And watching them is a pleasure

Rhythm

Reggae boyz going the extra mile
With moves that is truly versatile
The chanting of our dedicated fans
Give the players the upper hand
Staying with the mystical rhythm
We know that we will be winning

Chances

Moving the ball within the grove
Our chances is much more sure
Soon we'll have nothing to prove
When our boyz execute and score

Our heart

Reggae boyz going the extra mile
This win will give us a great smile
Soccer we love with all our heart
Playing the game down to an art
Performing their best is ingrain
Capturing the trophy is their aim

Hardship

Corrupted
Empty promises will diminish with the ongoing of time
It has no footing in a world that is searching for daylight
The smoky eyes that love to twist things for a lifetime
Will end up with a corrupted outcome and blistered spite

Take from
When you take from many and then give to a chosen few
Soon, lesson will show you many signs which is not new
You can only cause hatred and egotism among the ample
It seems you've enjoyed whoever you viciously trample

To belittle
I know you feel like a king with great position and power
With intention to belittle those you don't truly care about
But all dictators will have to face a life that is truly sour
Why deflating all sense of moral duty that will only shout

Diamond spoon
Waiting for a diamond spoon to make us happy and strong
Is a risky obsession we should never embrace then prolong?

Same cage
Low wage will finally put us all in the same cage
The richer and the poor will be at the same stage
In a few years the balloon will burst into the air
Then so-call richer anxieties, truly beyond repair

Liquidated
Finally getting a taste of what they have created
Still hasn't a clue who they have now liquidated
Caught up in a world of noxious self-indulgence
All fate is sealed and they cannot kill the evidence

Own tip
The sharpened sword is a long time in the making
Fallen on their own tip, will be no mistaking
They've sowed the seed of hunger in many places
Now their existence will have no related traces

Near future
A new world will be introduce in the near future
With human beings who care and respects nature

Be steady

Don't get too excited, cause your composer won't be united. Tried to be steady, and for you, life will be ready. Cool down your temper, and then you'll see the world you want to enter.

Pay attention to the little things, because joy and sweetness it will surely bring. Keep life simple and straight; remember always to keep the faith.

Destroy

With this suffering, we now can hardly face life situation. Working days and nights, hoping everything will turn out right. Today greediness pretending to have remorse, but they will persecute you if you don't follow the course. Sitting comfortable with the remote, controlling how loud we should shout. Greed is a hell of a thing, it destroy all love and bring forth suffering. The day must come when this crime of exploitation will be exposed, and then the world will plant a simple kind of genuine rose.

Renew
Today, we are aggressively over work
While business people take all the revenue
Now we can only function by guesswork
Our brains are drain and it can't be renew

Design
Each idea is design to keep you cage up
In a tight space with no room to breathe
They are really a master of this lineup
As more people will have to take leave

Worldwide
Together they have a worldwide plan
How to strip the working people's flight
Killing their esteem like a pack of clan
With no real remorse eventually insight

Health
Sadly, after they have acquired their wealth
Some will realize all they did want is health

Moral duty
As they feast upon the destructive fruit
Complimenting each other of its sweetness
The whole world is in chaos
Because most people have lost their moral duty

Dread
Conscience is in decline
The guidance to want it all makes them ever so blind
Many Blood will be shed
Our remaining days going to be Utmost dread

Lies
Lies are a permanent fixture in most every day living
They will despise you when you talk of giving
A multitude of discomfort they'll impose upon us
Only because we don't want to join their slumbering struts
As we are living in the light, we shall forever do what is right

Dismantle
Don't wish to be another
You might not like what you see
Your wants may seem too big to handle
Then all happiness will be dismantle

Illusion
Most people like to pretend what they are not
And somehow always hiding the fact
Flashy clothes fancy cars
Ah the beautiful house and don't forget about the magnificent boat
All this self-importance is just an illusion

New start
Worry not about what your neighbors have
With peace within your heart, you can make a new start
As time catches up to us, we'll have to put our energy where it's mostly needed
Remember wishful thinking must be heeded
Don't wish to be another; you might not reach your real endeavor. The need to share these tips makes me overwhelmed; it's certainly known that with really smart work you too can be at the helm.

Don't waste
Where there's no room to ever truly grow
You've got to move on before tomorrow
Don't waste your strength on a promise
Which is never willing to compromise?

Stifled
Why be stifled with someone's obsession
While building their hurtful transgression
You cannot slow down their unruly want
When surrounded by their faithful servant

Sour
Knowing they can do as they so desire
For workers, nothing will ever transpire
We're at the mercy of those with power
I must leave before life gets really sour

Counts
It's always what we do, that really counts
Start slow then move unto bigger amounts

Weary shells

Evening comes and there's no energy left for us
Our weary shells will collapse on the sofa
Our pocketbook is getting thinner
And so-call cut above is ever so richer

Upper class

The show off from the alleged upper class
Pretend that life is very much normal
But how can we forget those whose bones have been
worn out by the greed of the low-lives. Until they have
been on the receiving end, of these gut wrenching
hardship they will totally ignore us.

To cope

We're not crying over spilt milk, but how can the world
last much longer with this unkindness. The suffering
person has fallen under a very slippery slope, now
they're trying the best way they know how to cope.

Mislead

Impresser and tricksters always have tricks up their sleeves
As they just can't wait to deceive
Today the world is saturated by imps
They'll go out of their way to look pretty then they'll mislead

Divide

For those who held post of power
They'll squeeze all information from the needy and their existence will be
devoured Look at most workplace throughout the world, it's ingrained in some
leaders to divide the working people leaving them with a mindset of helplessness

Lowest

Professional agitators are really on the loose
Carries out the work of their recruits today
Stooping to the lowest you will see produce
With laughter loud and strong busily at play

Destroy

Pretending to be one thing, but it's another
Watching every move that's on the floor
Rushing in the office to cross and smother
Whomever they can destroy and deplore

The tattle

Many perks has been offered to the tattle
It's now on a roll of never turning around
A life of self respect they have dismantle
So sad it is, to see peoples mind confound

Cruel steam

Soon they will run out of their cruel steam
With the directors laughing to the extreme

Fruitless fake

It's a mistake to partake in fruitless fake, that kind of road will lead to insomnia and we'll never be awake. So sweet to live in a world of realness, it makes our heart feel light and refresh.

Truth

Much energy has been burn trying to locate the truth, yet we know it's worth it, in whatever we do. We'll spend our time in a no win situation, but trusting the truth we'll find the real liberation.

Contradiction

One-self will be revealing, no matter how hard we try. Living in contradiction, you must face a life of indignation. Self-exposure has the evidence; it slashes all mark of deception. Don't go trying to trick whose eyes you've already open, they do remember what deeds you've done and words you've spoken.

Real you

Doesn't matter what we do, behind us we always leave a clue. As we are not perfect beings, we sometime carry out unwanted foolish scenes. Whatever the circumstance, there is no excursion. After you've given the light on the real you; don't go pointing fingers on anyone who disapproves of you.

Smarty pants
Workplace bullies are in every workplace
They are lazy smarty pants in every case
Knowing everything which does not exist
Yet they persist with insult that they enlist

Weary
Travelling on a road that leads to nowhere
Wasting their energy causing surplus fear
Keeping you on edge every step of the way
Interfering with your weary nerves all-day

Certified
We shouldn't allow these empty agitators
To become certified unlawful instigators
Now is a great time to expose their intent
Before they cause another unkind event

Duel
Derailing other workers livelihood is cruel
Remember, it comes back mighty like a duel

Greedier
Co operational leeches sit back and seize their feast.
Today they are getting greedier, sucking the blood of the needier.
Some of us two jobs we have and slowly our prudence they'll rob.
Every day, new laws are created to keep the suffering class under
Wraps

Signs
Politicians and cooperation's togetherness are at their
Best, as the working people suffer every day. These leeches are
Over-swollen and about to explode, clearly we can see the signs of
Blood which will be splattered all over the dying world

Bribe
Hurtful overseers turning their head the other way, accepting bribe with
No regret. These greedy leeches don't know when to take a break
And that will be their biggest mistake

Heartless
When they latch onto our livelihood they will never let go, until our life
Exist no more. How much longer can they lie to the hurting people?
Soon these heartless beasts will be exposed to the unlit dungeons forever

Sunshine
Don't get connected with some old broken down work place, they'll steal from you your vibrant life. It is a world of difference when you are away from the smoggy grimes. Take a day off from work, catch the sunshine in its real glow, enjoy the refreshing oxygen, and listen to sweet music of many birds.
Then only will you realize what you've been missing? While you were slaving for the greedy cheap bosses, they will be outdoors enjoying what nature has to give. With this tight-fisted paycheck our heart said to stay at home, then we'll remember the bills have to be paid.

Remind
Got to remind our self we are not making enough money to live at ease, but just enough to keep our heads above the violent flow. As we try to shed some light on the situation, self-styled superiors will gang up on us and persecute us in every hurtful way.

Suffocate

As he turns to a knob of greed
Peoples livelihood he have suffocate
Now he'll sow only his unfertile seed
After making deals only he can relate

Safety

Pretending there is no safety issues
While the workers life is in danger
His trust no longer defend our issues
To us, he's truly a deceptive stranger

Change

Could tell when a rep has change
They totally ignore your concern
Moving closer to the bosses range
All his devotion has been adjourn

Token

It's sad to see years of trust broken
As you have accept the hidden token

Cold-hearted

After twenty-five years of excellent work, they received a useless plaque with nothing else to go along with it, except a thank you note. Only cold-hearted people would conceive of such cruel scheme that destroys the workers esteem.

Displeasure

 A total humiliation as the workers is very much partially awake. A big celebration is going on, but the workers cannot hide the displeasure from their inner-selves. A barbecue they say is free, but the burgers are burnt in the third degree.

Deceptive

Starting out they have a lot of firepower, but after a few bucks reach their pockets the flame is no longer there. With a deceptive mandate, they promise to be on our side but in our case, their two timing faces, we'll not escape. The fat is coming from the other side, and they will do anything to abide.

Suffered

A life style of so-call upper class in their case must be maintained, doing what the companies ask they'll not refrain. Many have suffered at the hands of the deceiver and crew, yet countless will be waiting to give them their Grammys. Betrayal is a permanent fixture in society today; all moral richness has slowly decayed.

Income
Poverty doesn't care who you are today
It will destroy whoever gets in its way
Doesn't matter which country you're from
There's no mercy on your skimpy income

Pretending
Most rich folks don't remember their past
They will block the past like an outcast
Pretending they don't really understand
Why a poor person is shredded to strand

Hardship
Some old people will never make it back
From the hardship that the rich has unpack
It's a crying shame the damage they cause
Yet with no remorse they won't even pause

New rule
Every day, new rule on how to take it all
Leaving the entire working people to fall

Nothing new
This isn't a joke; work place that doesn't practice morality bound to give you a stroke. Heart attack is nothing new, because they don't care how much extra work you do.

Perished
You'll work forty-five years and when it's time to retire, no one really cares. Workplace principles have perished a long time ago, now greediness is on the go. Isn't that a shame, money is the almighty ruler, ruler of these evil dwellers?

Over whelming
The uncertainty of a temp is over␣whelming. We don't know where we'll be tomorrow, and it seems time won't let us recover. You don't have a life of your own; as they control your energy in every situation. Fulltime employees look at you with a scorn, as if they are better and more in demand

Foundation
A solid foundation is hard to be constructed when the oppressor's goal is to keep your dream unfulfilled, most of us will fall by the wayside, but it's our duty to pick up ourselves and strive to survive. Have to work with the time we have, it must be spent wisely every moment that's allowed

Clutter
Work-place stress can leave us in distress
Destroying our lives in every way we live
Lead us in a big clutter making us jobless
With zero to give, it breaks our initiative

Be alert
When some place is going dead, be alert
Don't ignore what's happening to you
Pay close attention to where it truly hurt
Only you care for you, and that's all true

Health
Our health is of no real concern today
The millions now crown king and queen
While the working person strength decay
The days of humanity won't ever be seen

Arrive
Now is the right time to slow their drive
Before all their stinginess hurriedly arrive

Demand
Work-place keeping us in line, because they think it's fine. The constant demand of authority over the wondering laborers, at times defined as we'll do whatever we want with them because their life is so unimportant

Dress up
Management of a two tier system will split up workers into groups and then practice a partied with a wholesome looking face. They usually dress up of course in fancy suits and other expensive wears, but that deceit always melted by the true light that sits on the horizon

Protectors
We'll be persecuted if we say one word, because they have protectors in every corner of the universe. Let me ask all you splintered looking inhuman pretty faces, who do you plan to fool forever? Peace and honesty must rule once more and remember soon it will be knocking on your doors.

Liberties
Taking your rights and selling it, they pretend to be protecting your interest. We cannot rely on our reps, they are making deals with our livelihood and our civil liberties have been swept

Discreetly
With twisted words you've got to be careful of, even you're so-call delegations; remember they are dishonestly on the other side. First management will discredit every word you say, and then your imaginary agent will finish off the job discreetly

Color
Don't be distracted by color, race or creed
There's nothing wrong if we are of a different breed
Some fools of the past and present too, have categorized the human race
But when reality is done with that, there won't be a tiny trace

Love
It's got to be painful trying to act supreme
Knowing it's all a foolish scheme
Why waste time pretending to be sublime
When all we really need is love, which doesn't cost a dime

Broken
Distraction is a minds game
It often leaves the instigator broken and lame
For all the control freaks of the limping globe
Soon you will be living under a constant spiteful probe

Manifested
Cooperative deception is manifested in a full time game, as the underprivileged desperately fighting just to stay alive. Their deceit no longer carries any weight, time has intercepted all hurtfulness and they too are now a little too late

Prefabricating
The most corrupted cruel brewed, Victimizing and prefabricating lies that the devil would despise. Their cry for more echoed across Downsview, by no means contented with the hard work we do

Security
Promises have been made to change all contraptions to full fledge automatic, but greed will destroy these no good grimes of poison before that will ever happen. Standing firm beside truth and justice, I've watch grown men and women sell their liberty for would-be security

Vitalizing
They instigate disputable news which the director cannot refuse. Once respectable inhabitants now they are like broken rejected tools. Vitalizing their wobbling ego, one by one they have all fallen by the wayside of corruptive emptiness

Unlawful
Misguided bullies taking over our everyday space
Telling us what we should and shouldn't carry out
They have been given some unlawful database
That will destroy whoever comes within its route

Destructive
No doubt they have been emulating the crowd
Who preyed upon the helpless on a daily basis?
Thinking they are superior and extremely proud
Polluting the atmosphere with destructive crisis

Cruel sting
As age settles in, all bullies will realize in time
The damage they have cause in so many lives
Will never be repaired, lasting for a lifetime
The hurtful cruel sting that will always arrives

Destroy
Life was meant for us to live free in every way
Yet the mean-Sprit of some will destroy our stay

Full conquest
Why put all your energy in another person quest
After it's over, they will pass you with no regret
Demanding is the tradition of their full conquest
Excluding you is very easy after you have sweat

Threshold
Its full time you start thinking about your target
Shaping it into life before you are unsteadily old
There will always be some need for that market
That you are withholding from the threshold

Bits and pieces
Your drive will come in bits and pieces each day
And it's your obligation to enforce its calling
No one is going out of their busy way to convey
What you should be doing or really overhauling

Move
It is your move to do what's now best for you
Don't wait for a lifetime deciding on what to do

Under the strip
Don't fall asleep and lose your only grip
When you've got things up and running
Doesn't take much to fall under the strip
Surrounded by people that's so cunning

Two-face
We tend to trust who is mostly two-face
Though we know they will cut us down
Denial is the root of our stressful case
In time they'll push you in and around

Existence
Even at our age, we all have to grow up
Keeping their ailing spoils at a distance
We must never give into what's corrupt
That would destroy our sacred existence

Alertness
Alertness is the light that guide our rudder
Take the time to be awaken or be smudder

All colors
All colors are the beauty of our life within
It makes the world come together as one
Blacklisting any one of them is a cruel thing
Now is a great time to let the alteration begun?

Harmony
Introducing words that destroy other nation
Is the most irrational decision you'll ever make
What's needed is harmony that extend creation
Instead of embracing distorted intentional fake

Phrases
They are so many different types of phrases
Uttering as we speak, at this tiresome session
Unwise people with spiteful uneven praises
Crucifying innocent souls with oppression

Enlighten
It's my belief that the world will be enlighten
As hate is toss out and love is firmly heighten

Elite
Our memories is at a high time low
The working people can't think clearly
With hardly any substantial rest to go
We're at the mercy of the elite, dearly

Easy pray
A global epidemic for clock punchers
Whose living depends on working today?
Those insatiable number crunchers
They see all employees as an easy prey?

Rejuvenate
There is no time to rejuvenate our brain
As they cut down on the akin work force
Our bodily strength under a lot of strain
While the dictators setting a new course

Overwork
The world is suffering from overwork
Then the receivers bask in the framework

First
Who told you that you are truly first class?
When so many people have no food to eat
Its true time you see the mess of the mass
That can hardly find some place to retreat

Second
Second class in your book is not so bad
You even go as far as embracing your lie
Making the most of your outrageous fad
As it grows into glut, that will be deny

Third
Third class people's nowhere to be found
They are in your tired lonely imagination
Which in time will surly run a ground?
With all your inferior ideas for separation

Coffer
Most of the world residents now suffer
By the hands that dictate the élites coffer

Already
Let's expose those heartless bullies
We've got enough problems already
Yet we all have to cope with fallies
That destroys us slow and steady

Attention
We must never give into those
Who's looking attention from us?
Can see their heart is tightly close
That deals with their crowded fuss

Damage
Only if they truly realize the damage
What bullying really brings about?
They would never induce the carnage
That will leave precious lives washed out

Satisfaction
It is not too late to change your action
Giving love, will bring greater satisfaction

Treacherous
Who have created this treacherous black hole?
Why isn't this hole another color of some sort?
Using words that sounds so bottomless and Cole
With no sign of a brighter living, only to distort

Damage
We are all guilty of this damage to the universe
Wanting more of what we already own each day
Not worrying about what we're doing and worse
The hole is getting bigger according to the survey

Seek
No one is willing to seek out a new way to live
We are depending on the old fashion life style
Destroying everything else with no real initiative
Not seeing the honesty which is more worthwhile

Rebound
Now is a great chance to turn around this rebound
Before we're devoured by our own cruel compound

Hazard
Lighter races want to be darker and tighter
While the darker races want to be lighter
Tanning in the sun is really a giant hazard
You will be burnt from the outside inward

Bleaching
Be satisfied with the color you've been given
Or under the awaiting ground you'll be driven
Bleaching is a very popular thing right now
But the casket won't be far away somehow

Recharge
Be genuine to yourself and the world at large
As you get older you will need to be recharge
Don't make sense to follow those misinform
Living real will keep you in a truly great form

Embrace
Life itself is the greatest gift you have received
Why not embrace the image that was conceived

Stealing lyrics
All matured crooks we'll throw the book
Steeling lyrics is their only true ambition
Growing old, without a strong outlook
They will die with a lifetime of detention

Factory
Complaining of what is not satisfactory
A flimsy short cut, their only way of life
Now, they will snooze inside the factory
No matter how they try to beat the strife

Laziness
They stood before us with rigid laziness
With such big words of humble deceit
Only waiting to destroy our sacredness
With betrayal which must sink in defeat

Smother
Talks of greatness they shared together
But we now know, they love to smother

Careful
Be careful of the dangerous icy slippery road
It looks like water but it's really deceptive ice
Many drivers will have to deal with this episode
Although they have truly tried to drive precise

Foresight
Will help a bit if you cut down on your speed
When you have receive some warning sign
Foresight is a very useful tool we all do need
Preventing heartache on the way to our deadline

Safely
Reaching home safely we all should hold close
Thinking about each other on the road is so vital
With no concern, most would die and expose
To the element of the recklessness that's crucial

Slow down
Doesn't hurt to slow down the vehicle today
Before someone gets damage in a dreadful way

Clientele

Payday loan is a killer of our development
They have no mercy on mistaken clientele
Lured them with easy money component
Leaving them all the way to excess in hell

Poorest

Setting up shops in the poorest neighborhood
Lending money with the flick of a finger
These poor souls would repay if they could
But hardship also set up camps and then linger

Hideous

Such an idea to keep the have-not in check
Is a hideous worldwide poisonous crime
People who are already up to their neck
Can hardly put together one single dime

Hurtful

Time to bring to light, these hurtful beasts
Before another become their pleasant feasts

Selfish flavor
The quiet bullies are way more dangerous
Working from the inside to your outer core
They will damage all that you have discuss
With a large selfish flavor that's immature

Opposition
When their cover is fully blown in a crowd
You have to be aware of their pity ambition
They will single you out, then acting proud
Destroys your being with foolish opposition

Distance
Keeping these bullies at a secure distance
Is always the best thing you will ever do?
Don't let them in close to your existence
No matter what you might plan to pursue

Laughter
Never mind the laughter that you hear
That is a mask of wound waiting to smear

Wandering sieve
I don't believe I have much more ideas to really give
To a place that is taking most of my energy day and night
Bonfire with all its hunger centric desire and wandering sieve
Bleeds our real nature leaving us with no self-worth to ignite

Noise
Can no longer stand the worthless noise from across the yard
That sounds like an earthquake and must be rightfully discard
This structure that endure for so many years is now declining
It's time to make up my mind to locate the right silver lining

Bias king
Waking up is one thing, getting up is a totally different thing
Have to pull up very hard one foot at a time just to get going
Yet greed will be waiting for us at the gate of the bias king
Creating all his wants before he gets in, in all that he's doing

Existence
Now the competition will decide bonfires existence at present
It would be wise to start building our own resources of resident

Quickly
Why cry over Monday's woes
Live from within and you'll see the open door
After four days of work
Why wait for Fridays to thank the creator
Monday shows up too quickly is our way of thought
But happiness isn't in Fridays only as we once thought

Concise
Wait not for others to make your Mondays refreshing
Be concise with your own doing then you won't be crashing
Mondays will be good to you, if you remember what to do
Let go of redundant habits and you will find life's real gem

Seekers
Don't give up your dreams of tomorrow-weary hearted seekers, or your days will be much bleaker. If you can't see straight at the moment, just wait a little bit longer and the answers you seek will draw closer

Spies
When negative forces try to penetrate your life's work, remember unconscious people always lurk in the dark. Deceivable spies will tell lies even cry right before your eyes, but they have only one intention and that is to destroy your willingness to keep on trying.

Undesirable
Don't give up when so-call friends or strangers make undesirable remarks; keep the pedal to the floor and soon you'll see the
Ultimate sparks. Your dreams are yours to keep, even if getting there is very steep

Sabotaging and deceit

Convincing

They'll bleed your heart with lies, putting themselves in a smooth situation. Their convincing dress up and painting is a masterpiece, if you give them a chance, our liberty they'll feast.

Uppers

Using money power, the so-call uppers will bring your self-esteem lower. The desire to be number one kills any chance of humane oneness.

Hardly

We have to take this type of abuse for a few dollars, which can hardly pay the rent, knowing that tomorrow, home we could be sent. There will come a day when these deceivers of sincerity, must face the consequences of their dishonesty.

Crumbling

Keep a straight head they say, and your life will be more pleasant. Honesty, love and respect are all out on permanent isolation, now the universe is crumbling because it cannot withstand this vicious indignation.

Daze

A working person these days, their livelihood is in a daze. Keep your mouth shut they stress, or we'll leave your brain in a big mess.

Egos

We shouldn't waste our precious time and energy worrying about the control freaks in the workplace; sooner or later their egos will be encased in a self-destructed case.

Reclaim

I have lost my voice to sadness
Now I must reclaim it at all cost
Won't be suffocated by idleness
While embracing my painful lost

Handle

Though the times is not of our liking
We must create a bridgeness handle
Crossing over to a more do-able hiking
Making our dream less easy to tangle

Learned

I've learned to lift one foot at a time
To rise out of bed in the morning
Have to remember to reach on time
Or my existence will be in mourning

Dim

When we feel our energy starts to go dim
Negative thoughts must be aggressively trim

Conceal

Don't be fooled by the suits, sometime they are nothing but self-centered brutes. Rolex watch, glittering smiles, don't watch that, it's only an attempt to conceal their dominated minded spurs. Cologne so strong, they better not walk close to a hive of bees, in all fairness their eyes will be permanently seal.

Rehearing

If we could see vividly what's behind the suits of lies, never mind the charming voice, which echoes past the truth that defies. So easy to jump to conclusion that the suit make the person, but remember they do a lot of rehearsing.

Lowly

The lowly pickpocket often persecuted, but the flashy suitors hardly ever face confinement. Have nothing against those who wears a suit, when they are brutes though, they should be exposed and rebuked.

Face

We'll have to face our ups and downs, don't matter how much we run around. Enjoy your ups while it sticks around, as some downs just can't wait to pull you underground.

Often

Most days we'll put on a merry face, but our happiness is in a guarded place. The new obsession now is to lie, as innocent people die. Every so often we'll see persons of truth, and then society will flatten them down to a powder like dust.

Fresh start

We are certain we'll make a fresh start in life, pay no attention to those that tries to discredit you in any way. There's important lessons for all who's in a meltdown, it brings us back to reality when we're facedown.

Why damage
Don't dabble in another person scadabble
Then wobbles your intrusive cruel stabble
Why damage the happiness of a stranger
Leaving them in a world that induce anger

Fix
Why not take time to fix your dreadful life
Instead of having a feast of ongoing strife
Why induce the stage with hurtful sorrow
When all the globe need is love tomorrow

Minding
It will take many a tries before they'll see
That minding their own deal, they'll agree
The only way to a better life is to retreat
From the constant sabotaging and deceit

Hearsays
Staying clear of all tricky hearsays today
Our whole being will be united right away

Ambush your speech

Don't suggest one single idea to a god boss; cause outside you'll be toss. These so-call bosses are control freaks; from time to time they will even ambush your speech. They are on the path of world destruction, and they won't stop until nothing else function.

Constant

The constant pounding at the lifeless souls sometime makes the hardiest wrench in everlasting pain. Don't know what will happen to the younger generations, we know this is only the tip of a huge iceberg. Some God bosses are being developed at a younger age, and they don't have to worry too much because those before them have already set the scheming stage. Whoever compromises with such deceit shall forever be in retreat. Where has the kindness for life went, seems it's been toss into the bottomless pit, where love and honesty can never be found?

Swindling

As he pretends to be our pal, he sold out our liberty as a full-time consultant. Representing his pocket, then ask us why the entire rackets. Swindling is crippling world peace; it ripped away whatever love that was on the increase. The sad part of this is they are more frequent these days, now it's in your face as they betray. With his ugly grin wider than a continent, he laughs with great joy looking very much over confident. I can see from a far though, he has enclosed himself with today's gluttonous foe. Carrying out such self-interest role, but in most cases it will take its toll. No need for retribution, in time our pal will face his own indignation.

Little ego
Don't throw another person under the bus
You could slip and damage your little ego
Hurting honesty you will never get a plus
It will spin you around with nowhere to go

Petty security
I can see those who embrace your cruelty
This type of life ensures their lofty living
For them, this serves their petty security
With always wanting without ever giving

Devour
Thinking this type of amity won't go sour
Some guards will be lowered with sadness
When time makes up its mind, it will devour
All those who has adored its mental idleness

Hardship
Why disturb another person's inner peace
When so much hardship is on the increase

Children cry

Some say you're bad, cause you've interrupted their fad. They will persecute you, in everything you do. Fabricating evidence, and then implementing it without hindrance. Worldwide suffering is going on right now, all love that exists they will happily plough
One want after another, they won't stop until we're under the weather. Hiding behind money and power, our freedom they will devour. Today most of us are turning a blind eye, refusing to hear the children's cry.

Oneness

Sturdiness comes from unexpected places; if we look closer we'll find it in all the right places. Criticism of love promotes an endless amount of destructive lies. It makes the entire world suffer with an open cry. Oneness is clean and sound; it keeps our hearts effectively sound.

Destroyers

As we tried to share these love words, destroyers of love will be taking aim. Straight forwardness is all we need; we only have to plant real foundational seeds. Watch out for those who want to poison our fruit trees, they will try to deceive us and bring us down to their knees.

Preside

Don't ever dream of being a shipper
You will be dangled from side to side
By many directors of the cruel skipper
Whose ambition is to preside and divide?

Certain

I'm sitting in the owner's boat all alone
As certain workforce are treated perfect
They will crush your esteem to the bone
So much so that you cannot even reflect

Cleaver

Playing with your reputation as see fit
Managers think they can do whatever
Comes to mind as long as they benefit
With the function of acting real clever

New faces

New faces trying to make their mark
By stealing your job with false remark

Trapped
Most jobs are like broken glass, so many control freaks still trying to attack the working class. In some cases it will take years to see that you're really trapped in a vicious circle, then after age fifty they'll prey upon you like a vicious mob.

Own plan
And so you are back in a corner, knowing one false move you'll be a goner. Society does protect these heartless beasts; at the end of the day they will be sharing your hard earn effort. It is great implementing your own plan; it provides self worth-with an open mind in hand.

Persecuted
The average worker left out in the cold, and these are stories, which must be told. Hypocrites having their way with hard working men and women, making Huge profits from the tiresome people. If we state one word we'll be persecuted to the deepness of their uncontrolled greed, because they have to keep their foolish security at any cost.

Concern
Where humanity are concern most eyes are closed to the suffering of the working population, but we're now wondering who'll be next, don't forget today for us tomorrow for you.

In your face
They will close the door in your face
Even after working twenty nine years
Today they are confidently bare face
With unwanted destructive spears

The loot
They will stuff the loot in one big bag
Then hop on their awaiting private jet
At their parties, they unjustly brag
Without any sort of remorse and regret

Remember
Won't remember your name soon after
As they settled in a life of greediness
Now you got to reach into your rafter
Making do with all this awkwardness

The light
Why wait until you are middle age
To see the light on the wavering stage

Bend
Little bullies will turn into big bullies
Bend the trees before they grow older
Or we'll be consume by wasted fallies
That can get worse as they are older

No sense
It makes no sense trying to be a friend
To your kids, when they need guidance
Reach them before they are apprehend
With a more dangerous tacky substance

Sides
Why take sides when they're wrong
You are only making matters worse
Dwindling their lives another furlong
As lawyers devour your scanty purse

Teach
For the younger generation tomorrow
Teach your children respect to follow

Preferential treatment

Selected few

Double standard is a killer, killer of all living beings. It snuffs out life itself, and leaves only the carcass to defend itself. Double standard is slavery first cousin; it cares only about a selected few, that's why we have to work twice as smart to formulate an escape.

Itself

What do I know about the chains of death? Well for one thing, we only have to open our eyes just a little bit wider and the truth will reveal itself to us. Most people will deceive you and wouldn't lose a night rest. Double standard is like a sword; remember it slashes both ways without remorse.

Why cast doubt

Why cast doubt upon our humbleness because we are of another color. We are people of the system, and then hating each other is truly devastating. They have taught us to kill all loveliness, as they direct their ungodliness. We have bitten the bait and now we don't communicate. We'll never succeed until love conquers all inner fighting, which is really uplifting. When we are more aware of this self-inflicting spur, then we'll cleanse the inner hurt.

Are one

All beings are one, so waste no time pretending to be the higher one. Many a wise jokes have been poked at the light beings too; which makes it hard to focus on their everyday errand. If we stop to think of the damages it does to our souls, we would not uphold such coldness that will eventually take its toll. All lives are truly precious, be considerate of what you do.

Fussy view

I'm sure those black sheep haven't a clue
What all the unwanted fuss is really about
People acting like fools with a fussy view
Damaging the world with long-term doubt

Happy

Whether you have a black sheep or white
They are very much happy with their life
It's not a smart thing to destroy and spite
Remember we all want to lose the strife

Scheme

The world is full of segregated scheme
Ready and waiting to ambush honesty
Extracting all colored pending dream
With suggestions of color and curiosity

Petition

Living could be a wonderful expedition
If the powerful, would end their petition

Ultimate dream

Factual beings need not make unnecessary scene; they are too busy keeping their whole being on their ultimate dream. Honest beings travel on a bright and narrow beam; if you look closely you'll see what makes them connect. It's a natural fact that sincerity must be planted, before everlasting happiness can ever be granted.

Racism does kill

Let's face the facts; racism does kill the seeds of most contributors of the world. Most inventers have had their inventions stolen and remodeled. Isn't it time we find out who are the true inventers, who have given so much to society yet in return have been subject to unfairness.

Attitude

A giving attitude can only enhance the world as one, why then a so-call lover of life trying to snuff out what is right. The world will never be one, until all human beings are treated as one.

So many colors
Why have you planted our market black
When there are so many colors around
To choose from, in every walks of life
That is more than adequately profound

Listen
Take a good listen to your suggestion
That you're better than another person
Spreading the ugly word of infestation
This is bound to hurt and then worsen

Existence
Most of us don't mind this speech
Which hitches our aching existence?
It does destroy our uneven reach
In many ways that's truly inconsistence

Vicious
Markets light or black will always work
Without your useless vicious guesswork

To be strong
Dark cloud is what carries the farmer's water
Without it, we would not be around for long
Living creatures needs it at their headquarter
That's where they get the power to be strong

Sunshine
Sunshine is very important within the merge
It gives life a fighting chance to spring alive
Without the vitamin d we would submerge
Under the weight of smug that will deprive

Capsize
Now is the time to learn from one another
How to get the most out of our existence
Most people want to capsize and smother
Whoever disagrees with a sturdy resistance?

Abound
The darker the clouds the more food abound
We only need a balance as it falls to the ground

Unkind brittle
Don't have to turn back if you see a black cat
Why fill your head with corrosive unkind brittle
That has no substance or value to your format
But only design to destroy others and to belittle

Beauty
When we think of color it should be of beauty
Imagine if there was only one color that exist
How would the world look with a blurry duty?
With just one straight line that actually persist

Unwanted
Today should be a day of true enlightenment
Yet we are busily creating unwanted belief
That diminishes our neighbor's betterment
In every way so that there won't be any relief

Universe
All cats are beautiful creatures of the universe
Why then some tired people are living in reverse

Black or white

Lie's, black or white is unsafe to our occupation
It destroys our chances in every complex situation
In whatever we set out to eventually pursue today
Making success difficult to sustain in everyway

They are

Time to see things as they are, without pretending
That everything is going well and really ascending
The color of a person don't make them trust worthy
Your mistake will show that their note is unworthy

Myth

We know white washing will last for a little while
Why then are those who cuddle that shaky lifestyle
Knowing the whole thing is nothing but a myth
Which bound to leave the masses of the world stiff?

Realized

Some of the younger generations today are enlighten
They have realized that all disregard must be tighten

Dark or light

Who cares if the horse is dark or light?
If it's strong and fast that's all you'll need
Why are you creating unwanted highlight
That's trying to destroy the whole breed

Spots

Horses with spots are beautiful creatures
They are as elegant as any other stallion
It's time we respect all natural features
Who brings home the vital medallion?

Love

The world would be a better place today
Sharing kindness and respect with all life
Embracing the richness of life everyday
With love that spread beyond all wildlife

Began

Why not give a ray of love to everyone
So a world of real contentment can began

Why labeled
There you go again talking about unwanted mail
Why labeled the mail black right off the bat
When there are so many other colors to avail
That could be used in any situation as we chat

Words
The world is tired of those who points finger
And not taking responsibility for their own action
Only a matter of time before we all show's anger
To the unhealthy choices of words with distraction

Respect
What's needed today is a full dose of respect to all
Who mail millions of letters of love and kindness?
Never minding what color they are overall
But a sense of harmony that leads to blessedness

Effort
Isn't it time we put more effort into contribution
That care for every human life with real solution

Disarm

Certified lazy people always have a plan how to defuse their dozing opponent
You're first encounter with the deceiving informant, is to disarm your fire power
Putting you at ease by being very respectful then giving you a mature compliment
Making sure they have one thing in mind and that is to make your life go sour

Leave

The worst thing about this, is that they work in a group, controlling the entire place
Oxygen that once flow freely will disappear over time, leaving nothing to embrace
They'll manipulate all the moving parts of the enterprise with no room to breathe
Finally as you become an outsider in all their devious eyes, you will have to leave

Smear

Misleading is their master tricks that they use to smear and slander the wounded
Then tries to enjoy the spoils that comes with the ill bounty, in all its deceitful lies
Yet we know whatever is built upon lies, is a distasteful life should not be tread
Everywhere you go, they will be waiting to perfect their craft like sadistic spies

Inserted

Generations of these corrupted paper pushers will stay intact until time is no more
They are carefully inserted among those who is willing to work without an uproar

Favorites
Preferential treatment destroys all foundation
Of the people who is in the same workstation
Not wise to play favorites embracing laziness
It will come back to haunt your petty in tress

Subside
Surrounding yourself with so-call security
That diversity of schemes will face futility
In due time, all falsehoods bound to subside
Under its weight of lies which must collide

Deceits
Standing from a safe place, I can see clearly
Your plans of deceits, starts to bleed wearily
Those whom you've trust with your solitude
Are now the ring leaders fighting to intrude?

Head to toe
Just as I have predicted many years ago
Cruel deeds will fall down, from head to toe

Deceitfulness
And then they all gave me my biggest push, in the direction where they wanted me to go
With their hidden agenda, half a dozen limping bullies crave hideously in deceitfulness
Receiving bribes of lowly promises that will never see the light of their awful tomorrow
How could my love and respect fall on so many deaf ears in one setting with selfishness?

Confidence
I must redeem my confidence to see a true way out of this cage that I will be deploy
Surrounded by all types of directors of constant poison, no time will be wasted to review
No one person can withstand these attacks with the hollow stamina that purposely destroy
The life of someone who only want to share the alertness of understanding to a lost crew

New strength
Wounded by the onslaughts of the whole ordeal, I've gain new strength in another place
It's about time I see that there's so much to be had, without their vagueness of authority
The time is now right to get on board of a different type of vessel that I can truly embrace
Where I have failed to complete what I have set out to do, it's time to seek true prosperity

Cultivate
Adversity is a compass with all the right directions we needed to cultivate our aspiration
Never mind how many times we have failed, we can recover with our vibrant imagination

Substance

Hope is the first stage of faith; it renewed our will to accomplish what we desire
When we give our chances room to breathe, it expand in many ways to achieve
Life itself can generate the substance that's needed to move on and truly acquire
All the things that will complete our wants and need as long as we really believe

Reasonable

So many distractions will creep on in, as we try to engage towards our education
Yet it is our birthright to ignore those who want to destroy our right destination
It is truly a great feeling when we can say we have done what we've set out to do
That will give us what is needed to enjoy life as we so want reasonable revenue

Revive

A great life is not just about wealth, but of a giving nature to who's in distress
It is our duty to remind those who needs help to rise again and kept on trying
When their will has been trampled upon and viciously rearrange by greediness
It's grand when we can revive another person's day with courage that's purifying

Humbleness

To regain our dream with humbleness, then see it through to total completion
Is the most gratifying thing that anyone can ever truly experience from creation?

Love and respect

Teaches
Love and respect is the most perfect mix
It quiet our nerves, asking nothing in return
Giving us daily doses of a natural fix
That teaches how to share with our concern

Honest
We don't have to step on each other's toe
To reach some kind of so-call destination
Been honest is always the right way to go
Without causing any unwanted infraction

Give
When we care for those who needs our aid
Our good deed will never be forgotten
Other moment in time, it will persuade
Strangers to give, then it will be forgotten

Courage
Only courage, to give all beings a chance
Can save the world from its sleeping trance

Upkeep
What is the point of living, if I don't believe in me?
I must remind my working pieces to wake and see
How can I get what I want if my will goes to sleep?
We must hit it with our might to give it the upkeep

Strength
It can only get worse ignoring our desire to excel
Respond to the push when it comes in a nut-shell
Age won't be your best friend as chances departed
We have to go all out, before our strength is halted

Fertile
Doubt will show its unwanted face for a while
But remember you have to show it, the way out
We don't have to embrace those who is hostile
Concentrating on what we should have is fertile

Deserve
A fruitful life we all deserve to partake and enjoy
Before returning to where we were first deploy

Mistaken

Some words might slip, which will end friendship. Don't take mistaken language to heart, in a moment notice they can depart.

Leeway

Hold no malice of yesterday, live in the new and don't wander away. Let the sun melt the hurt that tries to stay, give time a little bit more leeway so we don't all become a sitting prey.

Heart deep

Laughter is good medicine; it keeps the doctor away. When your troubles seems to be heart deep, take the leap and no longer weep. Give laughter a chance when other techniques become too expensive, soon you'll see there's no reason to be defensive. When life's dragging you under the raft of submission, ease back and catch a breather. Laughter is sweet; it makes bothersome feelings stay away. In all cases anger is destructive, but laughter is so much more constructive. Better start laughing at what irritates you, cause heart attack and stroke won't feel sorry for you. Please do the right thing, and let laughter in.

Pleasant tune
Love is a true candle of life real liberation
That will never go out of style any time soon
We must respect others without classification
Then the whole world will play a pleasant tune

Creed
When we take time to see the plight of others
It teaches the essence of every persons need
We should all give to our sisters and brothers
Whether they might be our race, color or creed

Gift
The breath of life is such a wonderful gift
It is not wise to dictate the future of any one
Let alone setting up road block so they'll drift
Away from their dream, then viciously overrun

Beacon
We all need a real beacon to guide our vision
From every malicious and wasteful separation

Purifies

Love is a healthy thing, if it ever leaves me, living wouldn't mean a thing. It keeps my heart in the right direction, and purifies my mind where it needs to be cleansed. Love has no connection with hate, that sort of life I could not participate.

Honeycomb

I sincerely believe the golden honeycomb that flourish beside the rivers of plenty, should be shared by everyone who desire it's sweeten contents.

Can-do attitude

A feeling of lightness comes over me, and a sense of can-do attitude started to brew; now I'll demand of myself a vigorous finish to my life's work. It's Friday and I don't have to work tomorrow at the nine to five, now I will devote all my strength to my own castle. Won't lie down and snooze all weekend, before we know it Monday will be back again.

Your own

You may say that you are too tired, but remember you're not too old to be inspired. How sweet it is to be in control of your own success. There will be some stress, but I'm sure it's easier to digest. Throw away other peoples negative thudded burden; start now to build your own rose garden. It's time to depart from unstable grounds, because the other side of town is really profound.

Look alike

How could the world function?
If all humans really look alike
There would be an injunction
With everyone looking ghost-like

Efficient

Have you given it much thought?
Why we are all truly different
Time to put away the onslaught
Then life will treat us efficient

End result

Too often, we hurt each other
Not thinking of the end result
It's not a wise move to smother
When we can live like an adult

Put away

Young children always teach us
How to put away the useless fuss

To say

I've got nothing more to say to you, you have dissected my trust, and then try to make me look like a fool. Now you're calling on the phone, yet knowing your lies will not be condone.

Honest face

In the future, won't be in a hurry to trust any would be honest face, knowing later on they will take me to a fraudulent place. You've divided my trust in many pieces then plead for an extension so you can complete what you've started.

Come and gone

A slender love, that's how I remember you, could never please you no matter what I do. Many years has come and gone; yet I still speculate in the thought of how life should have been. Before I was naturally strong, today much wiser but time's slipping along.

Peaceful

I'm searching for a peaceful kind of life, one that doesn't contain this multitude of strife. I do believe it might be a very long wait, especially if her honesty doesn't really want to participate.

Grace

Woman of such splendid grace, it is you that I seek, because you're so candidly unique. You are truly clear-minded and fresh, you keep my mind workable refresh.

Natural spring

You're just like the purified water that flows from the natural spring; your moral approach is a wonderful thing. Our love is from the ground up, and then it must be care for with an everlasting touch. Won't gravitate to some unreal lover, with you, I'll stay until my life expire.

Spunky persona

Your cordial love is what I seek, and I know your loyalty will be mine to keep. Won't fall asleep this time, my eyes are truly open and receptive to whom is real. Her spunky persona is what I require, that I can build my fire much higher.

Potency

She brought an outstanding amount of potency that keeps me on my toes. Your love needs no additives to brighten our life, it comes with its own remedy and it works day and night. Enough tears have showered my eyes before, but with your new love I'm willing to reopen the wedged door.

Shatters doubt

Focus on what you really love to do
It will give you the tools to pursue
All the things you ever thought about
With added support that shatters doubt

Up to par

There's nothing that can hinder love
It can wipe away thoughts to shove
Bring you up to par with a doing type
Crushes ones destructive uneven hype

Reunite

When we think of a real world of giving
It gives us the power to keep on living
Show us how to fix our dreams beyond
Reunite family so they will correspond

Right road

When we keep our mind on the right road
We will always have room for another load

Chosen

When distracted from my devoted love, I have to remember that you're the chosen one. When my strength shuts down, the thought of you makes me want to carry on. I don't want to be away too long; must get back to sing you your favorite song.

I can see

The direction of our journey together is really clear, with this road map of true guidance; I'll be under your loving spell. I can see where you have included our happiness as one, then why wait for this flight to begin.

Careful

You are as sure as the morning sun, with positive energy in abundance. We must be very careful of pretentious friends; I know they only want to see our loving relationship end.

The key
Love is the cure for our aches and pain
So don't go causing any more useless strain
Only love has the key that will set us free
As long as we are willing to change and see

Little while
We may be upset at someone for a little while
Then remember that hate will never be fertile
The desire to breathe love into anger everyday
Is the only way to guide our sanity to truly obey?

No one
Never mind who is pushing unwanted fires
Time to snuff out all the oxygen till it expires
No one has to join other people's immorality
Causing unrest, then hurtful surplus fatality

Pure
Love is as pure as our young children of today
That knows not of hate but real love and play

Deceptive lure

Your love for me is just a distant memory. Things you use to say and do don't happen anymore. Now that you are on your way out, don't expect I'll be nibbling on your deceptive lure.

My heart

We have tried to make it work, but your hidden lies were too close for comfort. Now my heart is wondering in a never-ending place, and I don't know if it will ever be found. I was too blind to see the true you, now I don't know what to do.

Chancy

Not waiting for anyone fancy, but don't need somebody who's a little too chancy. So many pretty faces out there, but in a flash all that glitter could disappear. Much work goes into searching for the right love, now I'll let nature travel where it so desired.

Ultimate task

Sometimes we've got to relax, and surely the light of our life will be a natural fact. When we pressure a supposed lover, the odds just grew against our favor. It's a mistake trying to impress with a monetary brass; it might just take you to the ultimate task.

Authentic
All life is connected in some authentic way from creation
That's why we should treat everyone with genuine respect
What kind of life do we expect with a dented domination?
When we embrace unending war with devious conflict

Be lit
Each life was created with unlimited love in mind for us
Why then, some people think it shouldn't be contagious
It is great what the world could be like, if we cared a bit
A flame of harmony will gradually and eventually be lit

Sudden splash
Can you feel the joy with a sudden splash of real happiness?
Did you touch the wantingness that makes you overwhelm
Then why not share it with strangers, with this blessedness
You will see the whole depiction when you are at the helm

Caringly
Love is the real master of time that created this land and sea
Then why not treat every inhabitant on this hearth caringly

To wed you

Novelene let me be the one to wed you, if I lose you, just wouldn't know what to do. So many times I have tried to capture your heart, but you would never accept my yearning desire. Meet me half way with your precious love; I will carry you off to higher heights like a punctual dove.

Gracious smile

The most gracious smile belongs to you; if you give it to someone new, my heart would be broken into two. Each time I see your beautifulness, my heart preserved your blessedness. It's about time you say yes to my quest; give me the answer that we both can digest. Woman, leave me not astray; because your authentic love I'm here to obey.

Intend to stay
Cousins are special in every way
Helping when we're feeling down
Their love always intend to stay
Even when they are not around

Their heart
I think of my cousins in what I do
Never wandering from their heart
Their love for me is nothing new
That's why we'll never stay apart

Togetherness
Now I have been away for awhile
That doesn't mean I love you less
Soon we will be united for a while
As time digs into our togetherness

Trust me
I can only ask for you to trust me
In everything that I share with thee

Awaken

Sometime our thoughts will idle for a while
Yet it must be awaken from its drowsy state
We all have grounds which is not too fertile
That's why we got to cleanse our rusty gate

Infiltrate

Much useless noise can really penetrate
Our mind when we are agitated with defeat
It is a great time to let our desire infiltrate
The stubbornness that lingers indiscreet

Don't wait

Only you can filter out the severe laziness
That is trying to take over your livelihood
Don't wait for a perfect plan to impress
Your mind to destroy the harsh falsehood

Serve us

Our thoughts was meant to really serve us
Why then, do we linger without a real plus?

Compensate
Love is the greatest equalizer that you will ever see
It cuts away all the surplus hate, and then compensate
The substance that is needed for us to see positively
Is in our doing that we eagerly cherish and participate

All have
Sometime thoughts of destruction will surely intrude
With harmony hanging upside, dangerously subdued
We all have to take command of our own life today
Not giving into the misguidance's that lead us a stray

Harmony
Love will remind us of harmony when we are down
Give us strength that we'll elevate above our sadness
Straighten all the things that should be greatly sound
Making life's adventure perfect without the madness

Put aside
When we put aside our differences, we are at peace
Then happiness will be our guard as true love increase

Clear to see
Clear to see that I'm the people's poet
Seeing everyday life as they really are
No desire like a sugar-coated puppet
Who tell lies to start unforgiving war?

Unstable
The world is full of unstable intention
No wonder we suffer most days today
Crooked hearts don't want intervention
That would expose their covetous way

Rustles
The rich rustles from the working kind
As if that way of living is so amazing
Time have a way of teaching the unkind
With all its artilleries furiously blazing

What's right?
Most people won't stick to what's right
They will agree with shortcuts and spite

Giving love

Life could be so much fun
Yet so much blood we shed
Giving love, it will never done
Time to look for peace instead

Row by row

When will we stop the blood flow?
We're dying all over, row by row
Look beyond money and revenge
Soon nothing will be left to avenge

Stormy weather

How much bleeding can we sustain?
Why not show love to each other
Before we all go down the drain
Just like a blazing stormy weather

Row by row

When will we stop the blood flow?
We're dying all over, row by row
Look beyond money and revenge
Soon nothing will be left to avenge

Overdrive

How can we ever survive this way?
With this much hate in overdrive
Our destiny they will surely pray
Making it so hard to really arrive

Row by row

When will we stop the blood flow?
We're dying all over, row by row
Look beyond money and revenge
Soon nothing will be left to avenge

Peace within

Neighboring children
Burton town, where Sandra and I lived, alongside Sylvan's Gayle town
Our energetic friends, neighboring children, Sandra, Mavis and Marlene
Comb and plait the grass that looks like real human hair, where we roam
Monday will be here soon and school will take the place of natures green

Shared
Before we go home, we'll share small portions of food that we've bring
Swapping every bite with love that we had shared since we were little
We'll wait for Sunday to come again, where playing means everything
Life without love was not recommended, as life can become very brittle

Mission
Kindness was the cornerstone of our existence in real living yesterday
Been four, five or six years old, only fun seems best in whatever we do
Playing was the reality of all kids who just want to be kids in everyway
Nothing could ever get in the way of our mission that we really pursue

Reassures
Reading stories to each other, reassures that our bond will make us grand
Then most of us disband, to discover our unknown future in another land

In the morn
Jamaica is the land of wood and water
That's where reggae music was born
The beaches is of warmth clear water
Makes you want to swim in the morn

Vibrant
The sunshine's full of vibrant strength
It wakes you up, early in the morning
Returning to Jamaica for a long length
Beautiful sites that so really warming

Replenishes
Can taste the mineral from the dishes
Pulsating substance it will distribute
Where I'm lacking it will replenishes
With so many different kinds of fruits

Creatures
Jamaica, the land of many features
Her love shared with so many creatures

Take flight
Let the waxwing sing; though it's early in the morning. Isn't it a beautiful sight, watching these magnificent birds take flight? Their song is enough to quiet your soul, when you are on a misguided roll. Lots of chicks to feed but they always find time to rehearse. Many visits from predictors will be ensured, in ten days or so flight must be secured. The waxwing is a beautiful bird and their songs will always be heard. Let the waxwing sing, because sweet music they'll bring.

So free
Songbirds oh beautiful songbirds, your songs make us feel so free. Sweet music of much flavor, your songs are of such quiet grace. If we would only let nature be part of our daily living, we would do away with all misgiving.

Refreshing strength
When I need some refreshing strength you'll find me by the river, where peace and harmony is endless. As the traffic cuts down on the noise, you can hear these songbirds from far away. Natural music is true and pure, they even sing for free on the steps of our door.

Like therapy
Birds are like therapy, they give us self-worth when all the chips are down. We only have to care for these birds with an honest heart, then how can anyone ever take their love apart. Songbirds are true singers of songs, so we must reach out and protect their fragile homeland.

True harmony
Go on now, sing whatever you like
But reggae will draw you in slowly
With its base and true harmony alike
Never straying from what's holy

Always rise
Giving I strength when I'm so weak
Reggae always rise to the occasion
Reminding us always to be meek
When facing all types of tribulation

To meditate
Reggae gives real time to meditate
To rise above the cruelty of life
Then send us on our way to wait
For the true essences of a new life

True giver
Reggae, a blessed music that deliver
Remind us that it's really a true giver

Fragrance

Walking down High Park, giant bumblebees vibrate the scenery as the blossom with fragrance fall from the trees. When the mist covered the beautiful flowers, expect the sun to retain their gracious splendor. If you look up you can see the birds and if you listen just a little, the sweet sounds of music will refresh your every steps.

As natures do

The grass they shape like a heart then just up above flew a flock of dove. It's a very hot day, but with all this beautiful flowers how can we complain in any way. The sun surrendered its energy for free, so we'll take it in and count our blessings. If we take the time to live in love as natures do, our broken world would be brand new.

Serenade

My neighbors of birds keep my company, with the most beautiful tunes every day. If I leave my home, don't know what I would do, surely would miss the early morning serenade and the midday harmony. I wonder how they could keep on singing, with such beautiful musical instrument. By the river I can be a little closer to the action, they even take off and land close by. There you can gaze up in the trees as much as you want and no disturbance will arise. Just the sweet sounds of tranquility, that flows across the pinnacle of trees.

Really relish

Breadfruit ackee and salt fish, is our national dish
Most home have a tree in the front and back yard
You can never go hungry, that's why it's really relish
Nowadays it is truly famous and must be safeguard

Grandeur

The fourteen parishes of Jamaica secure its splendor
With love and all the trimmings that make it so grand
All visitors want to taste this national fruit of grandeur
That is making waves in our harmonious Reggae Island

Tree of life

A beautiful sight to behold when the sun rises at dawn
It nudges the ackees to open its pods, so it can be eaten
Our beloved fruit we treasure, it gives us power to spawn
Making survival easier, as our strength won't be beaten

Best treat

Jamaicans love this tree of life; it is the world best treat
That our country adore with its gratitude that is complete

Clean water

Let the trees grow, if we pull up the root there'll be no fruit. Help it along, and then for sure it will be big and strong. Today the vegetations struggle to stay green, without clean water they won't stay serene.

Staying alive

Nowadays we brag about our beautiful coast, but if we don't care about it, tomorrow it will be toast. Some of us despise the trees that keep us alive, yet we equally love to breathe healthy and staying alive.

Endless

Take time to appreciate the sunshine, the energy is of such warmth delight. Without the sun nothing would grow, so this awareness on you I bestow. Go forth and plant your garden of love, then tomorrow we'll all enjoy the fruit of eternal love. If we could only feel the power of endless giving from the sun, all this useless fighting would soon be done. Nature is so real; there are no corruptions even on a small scale. All living things would cease to exist, if the sun fails to make an entrance. We are pretending that the sun is not important, our ignorance had covered our senses, and our inner world is under attack. Soon we won't be able to see where we're going, if we refuse to comprehend what we are doing.

Vibrant and strong

Our natural resources are second to none in Africa and the Caribbean land. Our minerals that sustain life are vibrant and strong, that's why our fruits have all the necessary substance. We'll never appreciate the strength, which comes from within our natural home-grown food, until we are away for a little while. Our seasoning is of such power; it still works after many hours. It is time once again to plant more natural food, with all this chemical injected provisions; we are bound to get in a much uncontrolled mood.

Proudly glitters

Our fly Jamaica airways with wings strong and free, is now in the beautiful sky
The black, green and gold proudly glitters all over the world and the Caribbean
Reigniting our pride once more with the Jamaican colors that will be multiply
Inviting you, your families and friends, to try our new birds, let the love began

Bonus luggage

Giving our Fly Jamaica Airways the strength they need to grow and be steady
Let's reinforce our wings, ownership in the sky; as we will be invitingly ready
The competition we got to keep in check by giving the most attractive package
Referral will give us a stronger grip to build our dream with one bonus luggage

Reggae music

Come on board with the Stimulating reggae music that will relaxes your flight
With all the love that you do expect from Fly Jamaica Airways now and forever
We are here to give you the comfort and deference you deserve like candlelight
Giving the light of love from the ground then to the sky with real care wherever

Love team

Fly Jamaica Airways was proud to be your trusted jet, for these few hours today
Spreading the word of your devoted love team, would be fantastic in every way

School days

I often think of my classmates and what they are doing now. Do you think I'm soft hearted? Because my mind wanders off into the past. Some of us pretend that we are too proud to talk about such things, but nothing in the world can compare to our earlier school days. The love we have for one another was truly immense. Today fame and fortune have destroyed all connection we had, yet tomorrow we'll wonder what happened to the love when we are really under the weather. Maybe time will change some of us, bringing to conclusion of then and now with a major lasting plus.

Embrace

Maica I can here you calling me, and I won't ever disappoint you
I will be back to embrace every bit of what you have to give me
Won't be fussy about the high life that most people really pursue
No desire to discard my natural place of birth that is so guarantee

Authentically pure

When I think of love and true happiness, maica is always close by
Years of my childhood I do visit, in my thoughts that do multiply
Doesn't matter what is going on in my life, maica is forever secure
Reminding me of her greatest love that is real and authentically pure

Yearning for

Have to take the fly Jamaica Airways pretty soon to my home land
Can't put off this urge of yearning for the land of my birth anymore
Cannot leave the blessedness that keeps me in the right upper hand
Got to take the initiative to explore the beautiful, alluring sea shore

The warmth

Yard is the best, the warmth you can feel through the atmosphere
Where by the food is of the greatest taste, that's in our hemisphere

Dedicated intent
A pair of birds moved in close to my window
Each morning they sing till their hearts content
Soon I'll be moving to another place to endow
My long term dream that is my dedicated intent

Natural muse
Their songs will stay with me to the end
Natural muse is therapeutic in all that we are
It gives the essence that our beings recommend
Paving the way for our wonderful lives afar

Songs diversify
Now at the new place, the ravine is close by
Even more birds keep my attention together
They flew from the trees with songs diversify
It's amazing how they do this, in this weather

New season
Soon new birds will join the brand new season
With colorful songs of heart, full joy of reason

Caribbean Host
The turquoise beaches of Jamaica's coast
Is the true essence of the Caribbean Host?
The greenish blue colors will invite you
To dive into the view that you all pursue

Sea-side
Miles of choices along the silky sea-side
Where you can stroll with a leisure stride
Coconut trees slanted along you're sight
Is a normal trend with a natural delight?

Sandy shores
Sea shells are plentiful as you can see
The beauty is in the beholder of the sea
Fruits that grows near the sandy shores
Has the taste of sand in its inner cores

Lifetime
When the sun sets in the evening time
It gives a sense of real love of a lifetime

Warning sign
There is no room to lose your hard earned vocation
When you work your way up to the very top slowly
Remembering the hardship of the whole operation
Will give you the warning sign to live more wholly

In reality
Stretching your spending very wisely in every way
Never thinking foolishly with your earned pay day
Time will make you reflect, before wasting vitality
That could have been put to a better place in reality

Kindness
When we earned our keep, we embrace life reserve
Every ounce of food we eat, we'll give much praise
Recollection how hard it was to earn and preserve
Living humbly with kindness is our openly phrase

My brow
I have kept an eye on whatever I owned right now
Watching with every sweat that drip from my brow

Vitamin D
For a moment I thought I have lost all my desire to persevere
My inner strength had stop functioning for many days in a row
Then realizing that vitamin "D" from the sun was nowhere near
I can remember as if it was yesterday, as my force return to flow

By example
Today I must put all my strength to the common good of respect
Leading by example in every move that I participate in, to protect
When we are very ill and it seems that our time is almost at hand
We start to reflect in every way that we should treat others grand

Lesson of love
Should not wait for illness of any sort to teach us a lesson of love
Right now is the perfect time to start giving with a pure readiness
Before life say good bye to you, in the most hurtful way thereof
It is not the most difficult thing to share the clarity of blessedness

Greatness
This is a moment of trueness to touch another life that is really lost
Can you feel the greatness of love that flows afar without any cost?

Natural purity
A beautiful flower for you and me
It makes our world pleasantly free
Real fragrance is of natural purity
Arousing the essence of maturity

Devotion
Love is what we need to practice
Not a half good, mix with malice
I will grasp the place of devotion
Promoting love, with real emotion

Amplify
When elation is in short supply
Our staying power must be amplify
Take a break from the uproar
Spend some time by the sea shore

Peace within
Life has moments of peace within
Demanding yours is a natural thing

Essentially

Most poets are more sensitive than they essentially look
They will take things to heart with deep unsteady sadness
It is not a good idea to use words from a spiteful book
That destroys the life of the innocents with hurtfulness

Don't rattle

Our aim in life is to share in a real sagacious giving way
With every thought-coated with holiness that will not sway
A poet has no use for twisted hurting assumption tittle-tattle
They rely on a true nature of clear thinking that don't rattle

Our time

The steady rage of our area, we have to face during our time
Is really a test of living we all have to go through to stay alive?
No matter the struggles, living induces on our brief lifetime
We have to keep a clear perspective on our reason to survive

Detaches

Most people will try to draw us into their useless deception
Yet it's our nature to detaches our life from a cold inception

Bits and pieces
Renew your tired brain and release the strain
Why dwell on wasteful thoughts that constrain
Now is the time to take control of your source
With the bits and pieces you can be on course

Useful stand
Don't give much thought to those who slander
Watch them from a distance like a bystander
You should put your energy to a useful stand
One that have a plan that you can understand

Groundwork
Most days you will be drain being over-work
Nothing will change without the groundwork
That's when you must start to think of you
Don't hesitate to pursue the things to really do

Activate
You must be the first to activate your desire
Then you will receive what you have enquire

The loving touch

Greater

Mothers and Sons have a unique bond
Their love is truly greater than you think
Much intrusion came from way beyond
And tries to break their unbreakable link

Lifetime

All know they are wasting their time
With persuasion of many spiteful bluff
Every mothers love is truly for a lifetime
And nothing else could ever be enough

Truly grand

The loving touch of a mother's hand
Is stronger than anything else that exist
Her unconditional love is truly grand
Always around when a crisis persist

Needy brew

Mothers are special in whatever they do
Forever looking out for their needy brew

Finally see
Denise B our true African historian, She searches for the truth wherever it may be, opened our eyes so we can finally see. She arises from her bed early in the morning, because she can hear our children calling.

Attribute
Woman you are of real gracious attribute, teacher of wisdom and truth. One who takes the time to share, only because you truly care? For some of us it's easy to lose sight of our Sheroes and heroes but you my dear, remind us to be aware.

These gems
We have listen to the African classroom on Tuesdays, with great knowledge you've lit our hearts and minds. We'll forever share these gems of enlightenment, even with our unborn child.

Your quest
Appreciating your quest for liberty and freedom for all, in our books you'll forever be walking tall. Only a few want to do, you are not only words but you teach us facts and what to do. Many thanks from one of your faithful listeners.

Real dedication
I know you can reach you're awaited dream
Giving all that you possess in real dedication
Making it your duty to persist to the extreme
It will give you the tools to your destination

Receive
Let not the hindrance of life slow you down
Try different ways to receive what you seek
The strong have the patience to stick around
That's what put them all on a winning streak

Elevate
Believe in your plans you've really set aside
Waiting on chance nothing will ever renew
Now is the time to truly take the final stride
To elevate all desire for what you've pursue

Required
Only action can ever give you what's desired
Go on now and sow the seeds that's required

Determine stride

General science is his greatest endeavor
He teaches with such a determine stride
Makes every moment captivatingly clever
Most of his students always leave electrified

Shall surpass

Pushing us to be really smarter everyday
We got to spell words before leaving class
Realizing his motive, I've learn right away
That my difficulties in life I shall surpass

Guide

His voice rumbles through the classroom
Commanding respect from all who's inside
His wisdom devastate all chance for gloom
Making sure his knowledge, was my guide

Skills

Grateful to be a part of class seventy two
He has taught us skills that was truly new

Justly request

Life has its true purpose for everyone
Now is the time to manage your quest
Let your determination guide your plan
With the energy you have justly request

Key

Following through is truly the only key
It gives us strength with our devotion
Procrastination can smash your entry
That's why you got to create a solution

Succeed

No one can carry the fiery torch alone
We all need real guidance to succeed
Today most of us are now on our own
Probing for the answers we really need

Achieve

By sticking to our plans we will achieve
Most of the things that we ever conceive

She enlighten
Empress Minott, our princess reggae singer
She enlighten us with words of assurance
If you are a season veteran or a beginner
Her aim is to guide you to go the distance

Can grow
Have met her once in the studio years ago
Could tell she has a whole lot conceive
To share with her fans, so they can grow
In whatever they've chosen to achieve

Message
Constructive works will always be on top
No matter how long ago it was created
The message of love can never be stop
It wakes up many of us, who are frustrated

Mission
Her mission will be completed on time
With all crucial strength working overtime

A winner
Thinking one step afar, we can be a winner
We can't leave success up to a close friend
Have to go all out even if we're a beginner
That's how we'll be able to truly transcend

True light
Always finishing what we've now started
Is one way we will be on the right flight?
Our objective should never be halted
Seeing the road of survival in a true light

Renewal
We all have to wonder about our life today
Then make plans for tomorrow's survival
Time will push us on in some great way
With strength that we'll need for renewal

Inspired
I will stake my claim on what I required
Then move onto new things that inspired

Genuine
Real kindness of today will never grow old
It lingers until genuine lasting truth disclose
Just a few people embrace this great threshold
That the world needs to survive, yet they oppose

Shares
I will remember you in life's plight in every way
Helping out in whatever trouble that tries to stay
In the course of living, life has its ups and downs
Yet a person that shares hardly ever truly frowns

Endure
Where ever we might be today or tomorrow
Memories of a giving heart, lingers forever more
Always helping with some unwanted sorrow
Finding answers for others so they can endure

Gratitude
This is a motion of our gratitude from within
Cause of your true nature, life has new meaning

Content
Not so long ago you have demanded from life
All the things that would make you content
We only have to pave the way from the strife
Then we'll receive all what's truly prevalent

Vital
Determination is a vital matter that creates
It has the power to bring us what we want
Never mind all the flimsy weak debates
Let no one persuade you that you can't

Persist
The first step is always the toughest to initiate
That's why we have to persist in what we do
To make waves in whatever we activate
We only have to hammer our plans through

Choices
Choices that was created from true kindness
Always persevered with complete blessedness

Nothing new

You have always followed through
Because you want to succeed in life
This reminder is really nothing new
As it removes all of the nagging strife

Fulfilled

Our existence can truly be fulfill
With the right kind of sturdy action
Never mind who wants to stand still
Not taking the significant direction

Endeavor

Finishing the vital chores conveyed
Is the most gratifying thing ever?
Remembering that to honestly get paid
We've got to be firm with our endeavor

Efficient

Today life will treat us much different
When we work more wise and efficient

Her natural
The consciousness of Queen Ifrica is fi real
That's what the world truly need right now
Her natural way of life can help us to heal
Then anchor the stableness of life to endow

Foundational
It only makes sense when she gives her all
Never diluting her purpose to really teach
Always following the foundational call
Sharing wisdom to those who want to reach

Sacrificing
Sacrificing her safety day in and day out
Yet won't give into any negative solution
That would make hesitation come about
She's Jamaica's queen of true attribution

Devotion
Focusing on what can be done in the present
That's where her devotion will be really spent

Dreams
Dreams are made of significant action
A casual act will never ever produce
The benefits of an accurate satisfaction
You are now ready to promote and induce

Can lead
We have learned that snoozing too often
Can lead to a life of lateness that crumbles
Never letting go without leaving us soften
But with this start we'll no longer stumbles

Bright
I will squeeze every bit of juice right now
From my new found agenda that is bright
With all the parts that is needed somehow
Must follow through with ideas that's right

Strength
Gaining strength that has the ultimate drive
Precious time won't be wasted in overdrive

Wholesomeness
She sings with a voice of true wholesomeness
Like a bird that bring message pure and clear
Such songs is of great essence for the trueness
When most wondering souls chose to be aware

Sunshine
We can feel the love of her story, in every line
It draws you in, deliberately with real sunshine
Doesn't matter if you have a really rough day
Her music will calm your stress in every way

Abode
Songs of teaching is in real demand nowadays
Spreading realization is welcome in our abode
The flow of harmony we will give much praise
You are an ambassador of life at the crossroad

Substance
Great songs with real compassion, do enhance
Our hearts with credence and loving substance

Your means
Get out of the red and back into the black
Why do you waste all that time off track?
Spending within your means is constructive
No need to follow friends who is disruptive

Insatiable
It will take a lot of preparation to figure out
How to tame this insatiable beast that shout
Living your own life is always the best thing
It keeps you consciously aware of everything

Straighten
Only you can straighten out your life now
Taking the steps that's needed with a vow
Life will not wait for us as we play around
It kept on going in spite of our background

Regular
Save a bit on a regular basis when getting paid
Building your castle, even if you are underpaid

Ambition
Educating the weak is her greatest ambition
Sharing real knowledge is what she does best
A real cultural reggae singer with a mission
Planting all trees with foundational interest

Fortitude
Without guidance, life would be truly tough
That's why she teaches with such fortitude
With every word, reinforce with loving stuff
To carry us through to the highest magnitude

Awareness
A caring sage with kindness you will agree
Always giving first in every way that exists
Lifting up the masses, whoever wants to see?
With awareness, way beyond how to persist

Strongest
Determination is always her strongest guide
It gives us the true power how to really stride

Journey

As I embark on my journey to learn
Much obstruction will be in my way
Have to retain my families concern
Then dedication I must neatly pay

Aspire

A compassionate life is what I desire
Giving the world a chance to be anew
Life is great when we all can aspire
In all that we say and continue to do

Kind heart

Will do my best to make you proud
As I pave the way with a kind heart
Won't express my giving aloud
That would smash my aim apart

Focus

Now, I'll focus on reaching out for all
For whoever might stumble and fall!!!

I'll remember

Love and kindness is what you have known for long ago
Now I'll remember all that you have done for me today
When life is full of struggles, we need guidance to grow
That's where you're message really takes root everyday

Giving

As time creeps in from our history that will truly unfold
We'll arrive full circle with the time that we have hold
Giving is a likely way of life which you easily realize
Not for one single moment, living or thinking otherwise

Caring

Caring hearts have the system to untie the mightiest net
We all need a lift some time or another in our lifetime
No one person has what the world needs, in one basket
To handle all problems that will arrive in the meantime

Empathy

Empathy is the source of power that will live evermore
Embracing it with natural love, that we can never ignore

Thoughtfulness
Thoughtfulness we should remember in our lifetime
It is a real treasure we have to pass on to our brood
Everyone needs a secure way of living all the time
Our continuation depends on our complete gratitude

Igniting
Thinking way back, life was so different from today
Most folks have the right kind of love to save the day
Igniting the beauty which is in most living creature
They'll go beyond their toes, to help out any teacher

Kindness
You are a person who will go the additional mile
Getting things done in every way that is proficient
Kindness paves the road for a harmonious lifestyle
It cannot be threaten by hearsay or any other intent

Openness
Openness is always at the forefront of your action
Now life has come full circle with true satisfaction

Giant lift
Remembering me is the greatest genuine gift
That you could ever really give your cousin
In times of seclusion, it does give a giant lift
Saving us from constantly fatigue and dozing

True love
This time of year we think of a special person
Who brought authentic just love for certain?
Occasions will never cut short our caring soul
That we've cultured with true love as a whole

Healthier
The joy of life we so eagerly share together
Is a real tribute to how we all should be real?
Making space for all people to live healthier
Is a loving way the world needed to reveal?

Beautiful
A beautiful life is full of happiness beyond
With the sustenance that is necessary to bond

Our teacher
DeLou Maureen Powell, Our teacher
Who was more than truly kind?
Taught us how to deal with the future
With foreseeable obstacles in mind

All students
Educating was her only mission in life
Giving more than what was required
Reaching out to all students in her life
She makes us truly strong and inspired

Knowledge
The real knowledge we have receive
From her so many, many years ago
Was a plan that she has conceive
That all students should really grow

Conclusion
As her world was without exclusion
I will now rest her sonnet in conclusion

To respond
Love and compassion always lead the way beyond
Your desire to help the less privileged around you
Make you much different with a mind set to respond
To the needs of who's making far much less revenue

Our journey
Through the short time you have truly been with us
You have given a lesson on how to live without a fuss
We all have to visit our journeys end finally one day
You are surly missed, as our love for you won't decay

Guidance
The proof of your love, you have generously provide
With all the care that any one person could truly share
Your legacy is of pure hearted guidance that's gratified
We will really remember the goodness of your welfare

Open heart
The essence of love is truly given with an open heart
When we share pure sacredness, we'll never drift apart

Rosa Parks

Rosa parks, she was a sweetheart, now we can drive at the front of the bus straight to all the parks. Ah, Rosa parks the woman who makes all types of fire sparks, we can now sit in the bus, left, right and center, all colors can be seated any where they chose.

Courage

Woman of great abundance of real courage, true liberty you have encouraged. We will show our gratitude forever, because you had sat down in the right position to give us the genuine strength to demand a life of equal opportunity and emancipation.

Open sea shore
We've taken the bus to alligator pond
Where you can see the open sea shore
The savoir of the sea sand correspond
To my current senses like never before

Ginger beer
There's a man with a horse and buggy
Selling ginger beer by a tall white wall
A distance from the beach it's muggy
Then the sun rain started to really fall

Sea grape tree
Roasting fishes beside the roaring beach
We sat under the beautiful sea grape tree
Love and happiness she perfectly teach
With kindness as the foundational key

Unify
Today thinking of those days gone by
Makes me search for a life that's unify

Truly essential
A loving heart is worth more than all precious capital
It is the hub that keeps the world from falling down
Giving with pure kindness in every way truly essential
Is what the universe needs if we are to ever be around?

Elevating
Watching you with your generous trait, was elevating
Today I will share it with whoever is into liberating
Time will never erase your memory in our lifetime
It's too precious of a gift to be wasted in the meantime

Beautiful hillside
Days of laughter, echoes across the beautiful hillside
That's were true happiness of life refreshes everyday
Living with great care makes the world truly justified
Creating what the nation depends on, is the right way

Evermore
The love you've shared with us, will linger evermore
In the hearts of your family and the future to explore

These attributes
Your love is my guide to the life I live yesterday and today
It prevent me from falling off track, with an urge to survive
The rule of living with equal love for your kin, won't decay
I will hold on to these attributes of oneness to truly survive

Morality
How could I forget your kindness that shore up my reality
With words of guidance that spread its light in all morality
Giving me strength to carry on with life which is so tough
In this day and age, whereby, a secure life is in the rough

Grace
A life that was filled with true giving from the beginning
Can only stay the course, fulfilling its significant devotion
Where would the world be without the grace of inspiring?
That you have given completely with all genuine emotion

Balance
Love is the balance we all need to prosper in all that we do
Embracing life, true clearness is natural with a fresh avenue

Favorite flower
Rosa, our beloved whole hearted grandma
Her favorite flower is the huge marigold
Life with her is like a world with pure ah
So much love that it will never grow old

Loving human
One of the most loving human being ever
Always have time to reach out and give
Regardless of the environment that hover
She will make room for people's initiative

Divine state
Sharing love was the corner stone of life
Was never a moment she speaks of hate?
Helping others especially the housewife
Always parted visits with a divine state

Honesty
Could never survive without her guidance
She guided us with honesty and tolerance

And now it's my turn

And now it's my turn, I'm resting quietly as you can see. No more worries over lives burden, a peaceful sleep with a closed curtain. Cry your tears of sadness; let it wash away the hurt. Don't be shy to speak of real love; it will heal your broken heart. If you are living on a structure that give, then we have shared the same pureness that will forever live. Take love home with no regrets, just remember life goes on and not to fret. I've gotten my share of what life have to offer. We all have to go when our time's expired, and leave whatever we have acquired.

Author's Note

To all my fans, readers, viewers and listeners near and far, it has been such a wonderful experience to share these liberating ideas that can change your lives, no matter what is the cause of the circumstance. We don't have to settle for the pittance that we receive for the back breaking work that we perform day in and day out, in some cruel unequal workplace. Once we start believing in our self, we can become whatever we set our minds to. As we all demand a better life, procrastination must be apprehended and sentence to life in prison.

Determination you will have to cultivate, gathering every bit of self-power out of its lifelong substance. Firmness is always a power house that has the super energy that every ambitious person needs. Persuasion is a great fit to all super sales woman and man; it will bring the real diamonds home. Action, we all need to start and finish whatever we have dreamed of then and now. Understanding the different ways to market our product and service, we will be ahead of the competitive world.

When we have self-respect, it is really the true guide we all need in every moment of our existence. The person who is totally aware of what is going on will be on top of his or her operation. Wandering can cause so many unwanted, uninvited self-destructive ailments of vicious diseases.
Carrying out our plans, self-confidence is a must; it keeps our drive in the right order of sequence. Our attitude towards the ambitious areas of success can be renewed with a more conscious outlook if we choose. When we see that change is necessary to cultivate a new life, it is our duty to engage in the things we so desire and bring to fruition the real substance of accomplishment.

We should put all the energy that we have in something that we can call ownership. It's time to give to ourselves, instead of giving all of our strength to other people who only care about themselves and their kin. Wake up now and rejuvenate your life with an abundance of a generous attitude that will give you what you seek and also give whoever helps you to acquire your dream. It's time to clear the clutter that hinders us from creating our destiny as we see fit. Always remember that a new day will bring new ideas and new strength in our time of needs. We got to set in motion onward regardless of the clutter that pretends to be our friends.

Author's Note Cont...

Remember it all starts with you and other compatible people will help you to finish your quest for a better life. To believe in your dream is the hub of the foundation that you will need, to build all that your heart is longing for in every way shape or form. Love, honesty, respect, kindness, self-confidence, a giving nature, are all from the same family tree, They will give you the power to acquire whatever you set your mind to, as long as it is within the capacity of truth and reason. One more thing you should remember, don't lose sight of your humble beginnings; divine intervention has a way of teaching the stinginess of scrooges that preyed upon the helpless laborers of the world.

www.ingramcontent.com/pod-product-compliance
Lightning Source LLC
Chambersburg PA
CBHW031139160426
43193CB00008B/189